Science and the Shabby Curate of Poetry

Martin Green

SCIENCE AND THE
SHABBY CURATE
OF POETRY

Essays about the two cultures

W · W · NORTON & COMPANY · INC · New York

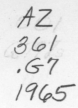

FIRST AMERICAN EDITION 1965
LIBRARY OF CONGRESS CATALOG CARD NO. 65-13525
PRINTED IN THE UNITED STATES OF AMERICA
1 2 3 4 5 6 7 8 9 0

To Jacques and Eva Heyman

Contents

Introduction

My interest in this subject began when I read C. P. Snow's The Two
Cultures, *in January 1960. But that book made such an impression on
me partly because it explained, or better, promised to explain, something
which had been in my thoughts for some time before. That was an un-
satisfactoriness in the book I had finally completed in the preceding summer,*
A Mirror for Anglo-Saxons. *I had been in a sense writing that book
for five years and more; it contained my most serious thoughts of an even
longer period; and it was therefore both painful and puzzling to have to
admit how silly some of it was. The ideas, the categories, the connections,
which were quite convincing when applied to literature, and quite illumina-
ting when applied to manners, became painfully hypothetical and even pert
when I applied them to political and economic facts – to official policies and
institutions.*

*It is not, of course, an uncommon experience, or in that sense puzzling,
to realize that one cannot apply one's best criteria, one's most long proven
categories, to some new problem; that one cannot, therefore, properly
speaking, understand it. What made this case puzzling as well as painful
to me was that I still felt I was right to judge those policies and institutions
by those old criteria; even though I saw I was wrong, that I made a fool
of myself doing so. One cannot, it's true, judge a political or economic fact
entirely by features of the kind I am picking on (this is what I would have
said); much of its nature must be quite alien to those criteria and proper
to itself, must remain quite unreached and unmeasured by them; but nevertheless this is something about the institution, and I can read it as a clue
to the institution's quality. Let us suppose I had condemned the House of
Commons as out of touch with modern England on the grounds of its
references to modern novels about England. Obviously, I would have said,
such references are trivial in themselves, in that they are irrelevant to
Parliament's main duties, but still they reveal, they can be made to reveal,
its quality of thought. Now that argument is by and large invalid; because*

one cannot estimate how much the trivial sign means, one cannot tell how to interpret it, unless one has first estimated the main duties, the general mass of the non-trivial activity.

This objection, which applies in some measure to quite a proportion of A Mirror for Anglo-Saxons, certainly entered my mind while I was writing the book, but I could not see quite how to accept it. I could not see quite how much force to allow it, and there was every other reason for allowing it very little. Because to retreat before it, to cut out that range of reference from the book, would have been a kind of abdication. It was only because I felt my insights (England's ingrown irony, England's fear of the present, England's self-miniaturization) were true about the country as a whole, that I was writing the book. That they applied to certain novelists and critics – that was quite a different proposition; one that was sufficiently well established already, and not one I felt any mission to re-announce. I was talking about a country's culture as a whole; that was my point; and I could not see that any less inclusive method would satisfy the rules of cultural criticism. How do your insights apply to political developments in modern England? To sociological developments? These would be fair questions – indeed, necessary questions – for my readers to ask, I thought, and I had to give them my best answers. I didn't fully believe those answers myself, but I couldn't see why I should disbelieve them. The logic by which I had proceeded still seemed to me impeccable; and the enterprise itself was one to which all my training invited and prepared me. If all I had to offer about certain areas of culture seemed or was grossly inadequate, that must be due either to the world's philistinism or to a squashiness in just my mind about which nothing could be done. There was nothing wrong with my method, so far as I could see; or rather say. For that there was was just what I suspected with the more sour and carping parts of my mind.

This was the problem I felt before I read The Two Cultures. It is not in any obvious sense one that Snow explains, or even promises to explain, in that lecture. I suppose I exaggerate even in implying that I saw a connection immediately. What I saw was that he had something to say about 'failures of the modern literary mind', which was one way of naming another aspect of this same problem. For A Mirror for Anglo-Saxons, though it dealt with culture as a whole, derived from literature and literary criticism. It followed the literary mind's logic, expressed its kind of values, *offered its kind of insights. The book's failures, if not personal, must be the responsibilities of that mind, that method. I had then been in some sense betrayed by my training, by my literariness, in treating that subject? Snow's thesis at least offered a line of attack on the problem.*

So for about four years I have followed up the ideas he put forward; and this collection of essays tries to make clear what sort of answer to that question I found. The pieces follow the pattern of my interests and activities during those years as much as anything more logically systematic, so perhaps I should say what those activities were. I read, of course, books about Snow's thesis, and other versions of the two cultures split, plus textbooks of science, popularized science, science fiction. I took evening courses in mathematics at Harvard and M.I.T. while I was still teaching English at Wellesley. I took the first-year physics course at Boston University in the summer of 1961. The following year I spent in Cambridge, England, attending the Part I lectures in Biochemistry and those in the History and Philosophy of Science. The year after that, 1962–3, I taught in a College of Advanced Technology. I wrote the essays on quite unparallel topics, and for quite different occasions, which reflect themselves in the rather various manners. I have not attempted to smooth out those differences entirely, because I thought their value in variety greater than their cost in continuity. The subject is a very multiform one, but I think my ideas about it add up to a fairly single statement, within which some variety may be welcome.

Acknowledgements

We are grateful to the following for permission to reproduce essays by Martin Green: Basil Blackwell for 'Lionel Trilling and the two cultures'; *The Critical Quarterly* Society for 'A literary defence of "The Two Cultures" '; and *The Twentieth Century* for 'English without Literature' (here appearing as 'Liberal Studies').

We are also grateful to the following for permission to reproduce copyright material: Lionel Trilling for material from his 'Science, Literature and Culture' and 'The Modern Element in Modern Literature' (the latter article first appeared in *Partisan Review*, January–February, 1961, Vol. XXVII, No. 1, pp. 9–35); and the Executors of H. G. Wells for material from his *The First Men in the Moon*.

'Science fiction' and 'Science non-fiction' first appeared in *The Kenyon Review*, Fall 1963, under the title 'Science and Sensibility'; 'A year of science' (December 1961) and 'Popularization' (January 1962) first appeared in *The Listener*; and 'Return to Cambridge' appears in *Proceedings of the Conference in the Study of Twentieth-Century Literature*, fourth session, sponsored by Michigan State University, 1964.

Science and the Shabby Curate of Poetry

When I find myself in the company of scientists I feel like a
shabby curate who has strayed by mistake into a drawing-room
full of dukes.

The true men of action in our time, those who transform
the world, are not the politicians and statesmen, but the
scientists. Unfortunately, poetry cannot celebrate them, because
their deeds are concerned with things, not persons and are,
therefore, speechless.

W. H. AUDEN, *The Dyer's Hand,* 1963

1. Two defences of 'The Two Cultures'

I

I begin with two defences of Snow's thesis. Although I don't quote from him often, and my investigations have not followed his ideas in any systematic sense, I don't mean to dissociate myself in any way from his original statement. I cannot see that the barrage of direct and indirect attack on it has invalidated a single point it made, with the one exception I refer to in the first of these pieces. The Two Cultures *still seems to me a very remarkable essay, for its local successes in argument as well as for its general truth of diagnosis.*

This book follows up only one or two of the pointers Snow offered. It has nothing to say about the new syllabuses and examinations we need to end our crippling educational split – nothing except that we do need them. It has nothing to say about the division between the poor countries and the rich, or the need for scientists and engineers to go out from the West to serve the needs of the new states. I have nothing to offer on these subjects that would be more than a rephrasing of his and other people's work.

I try to develop only some points from his early sections; the arts man's ignorance of science and vice versa, the ideological connection between science and modernity and the future, between the humanities and nostalgia and the past, the hostility the people on each side of the split feel for the other side, the invalidism this wound causes in the general educated consciousness; above all, the new complexity all this reveals in the idea of culture. In fact, even within this division of the subject, I have gradually found myself concentrating on the arts man's ignorance and hostility, the arts man's idea of culture. Only in this subdivision did ideas of my own seem worth defining and developing.

In other words, this book is concerned only with those aspects of The Two Cultures *which constitute a problem for the literary man as such, as a criticism of the literary culture as such – for being intellectually and morally limited in some significant sense. It is hard to guess at what could be called the received opinion within the literary culture itself on the subject of its own limitations. 'What's the use of going into that?' probably expresses the average response as well as anything. 'The point is their limitations, not ours.' The Auden sentences I quote as epigraphs represent a much greater than average consciousness of such a problem, and frankness about it. In its nineteenth-century, Punch-cartoon way, that image of the curate among the dukes expresses a great deal acutely and generously; and complexly.*

'A drawing-room full of dukes', I take it, does not suggest only the wealth and power of the occupants, the actual acreage of which they are landlords, but a certain natural majesty, a superiority in size, ease, calm (possibly at worst an ox-like calm), to the curate who has strayed in there. But it is a complex image, because I think one cannot read it as simply humble. This curate surely sees his shabbiness as a sign of a spiritual superiority. He sits mum among the dukes, musing over camels that cannot get through the eyes of needles, and rehearsing to himself the parable of Dives and Lazarus. Despite the very English atmosphere, this is more like Bernanos' curé de campagne than Mr Collins.

At all events, the two responses to Snow's argument I consider here decline to discuss any limitations or weaknesses there may be in the literary position. They bend all their efforts to disposing of the man who alleges these weaknesses. I had to convince myself that these rebuttals were invalid, of course, before I could proceed to act on the original recommendations. But that 'before' was a matter of logic rather than of chronology, for I had begun my attempt at re-education in 1960, reserving only final judgement. And in answering these rebuttals I found I was acting on those recommendations, was corroborating and appropriating some of the ideas in the Rede Lecture.

A literary defence of 'The Two Cultures'

IT is now nearly three years since C. P. Snow delivered the Rede Lecture that was afterwards published under the title of *The Two Cultures*. F. R. Leavis's recent attack on him and it owes some of its popular success to that lapse of time; because during those three years a fierce irritation has gathered among British 'intellectuals' (people who teach, or would in America teach, at a university, let's say) at the publicity given to Snow's thesis. This irritation is to be found among scientists as well as among humanists; there is no name to equal Snow's as a signal, at a university party, for every guest to get out his malice and all together start enjoying themselves. And yet – quite apart from the moral dignity of this behaviour – there has been no answering of his thesis. Dr Leavis's Richmond Lecture offers the best chance so far to continue (or rather to begin) the debate.

Dr Leavis's attack is concentrated on Snow's personality, manner, tone; claiming that these constitute a context for his propositions which fills out the meaning of his abstract nouns, his compressed judgements, his sweeping metaphors, his passing allusions; claiming that this context defines those meanings as confused, empty, and vulgar. He describes Snow's tone as one that 'only genius could justify', accuses him of a 'genially "placing" wisdom' that condescends to the rest of the world, of seeing himself as a seer and a sage; while supporting these pretensions Leavis finds only a 'crass Wellsianism', a 'swell of cliché', an 'embarrassing vulgarity', and an 'intellectual nullity'. Snow is, in fact, the type-product of as well as spokesman for a civilization which has lost all cultural standards. He literally does not know what words like culture and civilization mean, and his discussion of them is empty gesturing. The two cultures thesis is therefore nothing more than an ambitious man's attempt to claim an advantage for himself; the advantage of being the only man on both sides of the split. This is the diagnosis, moreover, of other of Snow's literary enemies in this debate, though most do not carry it so far, or, of course, so publicly.

The first thing to realize is that this is an isolated and belated skirmish in a larger battle. Leavis gives us the clue in his phrase 'crass Wellsianism'; and, later, 'neo-Wellsian'; he describes H. G. Wells as Snow's spiritual father and Bertrand Russell as his paradigmatic hero. He accuses Snow of misunderstanding, dismissing, disliking, all the great creative artists of twentieth-century literature; of not knowing what literature today is. (It is partly on these grounds that he can, later in the lecture, accuse Snow the novelist of not knowing what a novel is.) In other words, he sees Snow as the last representative of that encyclopaedist movement of the Twenties and Thirties in England which was one of his own early enemies. A movement dominated by Wells, Russell, Shaw, the Huxleys, etc., the spirit of which was summed up in Wells's three huge compilations, *An Outline of History*, *The Science of Life*, and *The Work, Wealth and Happiness of Mankind;* a spirit of broad general knowledge, national and international planning, optimism about (or at least cheerful businesslike engagement with) the powers of contemporary science and technology, and a philistinism about the more esoteric manifestations of art and religion. Behind it we can see the (much grimmer) figure of Herbert Spenser. For Leavis, this spirit contradicted his own preoccupations so completely that it amounted to a betrayal of every cultural responsibility, announced an ignorance of what culture is, and literature, and history. But it is possible for us now to be glad he felt that, and that he defeated 'crass Wellsianism' for us, without ourselves feeling that all Wellsianism was 'intellectually null'.

For us now that movement is so completely in the past that we can respond with free appreciation to its zest and scope of interest, its fund of common sense, its all-round responsibleness. It is hard, in fact, to remember how powerful it was, and that it could be a threat to literary standards, so complete has been the success of the minority faction of the time. People in England can now think of the Thirties as the time of the publication of *Scrutiny*. For the last ten or fifteen years the study of literature, and to some extent the general intellectual climate, has been increasingly dominated by a movement very largely antithetical in tendency. A movement which insists on narrow intense knowledge (insights), on the need for personal freedom within the best-planned society, on the dangers of modern science and technology, on the irreducibility of artistic and religious modes. This movement also has its limitations and dangers; and it is now so generally triumphant that these become important. Leavis has a point in calling Snow's style 'neo-Wellsian'; that helps us to understand and estimate his ideas; but by the same warrant his own style can fairly be called 'neo-

Jamesian', and he must submit to an equal, though opposite, broad pictorialization, as 'aesthetic' in his attitude to culture. The quarrel between Wells and James becomes an apt paradigm of some aspects of the present confrontation.

This paradigm, this general setting, does not in itself determine, of course, the validity of Leavis's attack. But it makes more plausible, perhaps, the contention that he has reacted to Snow's tone as a bull to a red flag. He has not discriminated; he has not registered exactly. Snow's manner, for instance, does not claim for the speaker that he is a genius. Quite insistently it claims that he is a plain man with, as it happens, a breadth of plain experience. He does not claim depth or intensity of knowledge; he claims breadth and simplicity. Common sense, not inspiration, is his keynote.

Nor is he pontifical. There is no priesthood of which Snow is the master, no esoteric training one needs to understand him, no dogma without which one is lost. He offers to make his ideas, his reasoning, completely available to his readers, and submissive to their judgements. He is no more a sage than a seer. There will be no disciples. It is precisely not among specialists and enthusiasts that he has any following. Pontifical, to Leavis, describes the serenity of Snow's tone, and the largeness of his ideas; a combination Leavis regards as impossible to a sensitive man today.

A 'genially "placing" wisdom' does describe part of Snow's manner; he obviously does enjoy his position of knowing more than either brand of specialist about the other speciality. But it would be a very ungenerous nature that could not allow him that enjoyment; and participate in it. For his is essentially a social and co-operative performance. He invites the reader to allow him his indulgence and to enjoy his freedom with him. Snow's tone is 'Let's agree to abandon between ourselves ("between you and me", perhaps) the safeguards of technicalities and indirection. Let's agree to simplify, to colloquialize, to run all the risks of short cuts. We're all shrewd, successful, simple men; since that is what we have in common, let's use that vocabulary – worldliness, careerism, gamesmanship. And let's frankly enjoy the pomp and ceremony our civilization imposes on successful men; it happens to be me that is getting the prizes today, but it might have been you.' There is surely no reason to find that tone, as such, offensive; in the present climate of opinion it is quite fresh, and, in dealing with such subjects, quite interesting; and Snow manages it to lively and subtle effect. It is a humility as well as a sanity in him that he accepts so fully his very difficult position; of representing the intellectuals to the outside world without being accredited as the supreme representative of either science or literature from within. His tone expresses that humility among other things. His position is, moreover, unique and self-created; he is not usurping anyone else's place; he is not speaking for literature to any audience Leavis addresses. He has created a new sort of social rostrum, and he is using it to give some large general truths the kind of hearing they otherwise never get. He can make educational and cultural affairs matters of national, even international, concern. Some of those who attack him perhaps prefer those affairs to remain private, protected, neglected, musty, because they fear a climate in any sense brisker.

The vulgarity, the nullity, the abundance of cliché which Leavis finds in the style aren't there for anyone who begins without the anti-Wellsian prejudice. He cites 'History is merciless to failure' as (and he says this is typical) meaningless as soon as you reflect on it. But it is a perfectly acceptable way of saying that at a given point in time some particular action may be so necessary that a failure in that will bring about total ruin. He says that Snow's contrast between social hope and individual tragedy is stultifying, invalid, and, like the first quotation, meaningless. 'Where, if not in individuals, is what is to be hoped for – a *non*-tragic condition, one supposes – to be located?' But again, it means quite clearly that what distresses us in social conditions can be put right by an exercise of collective will-power and intelligence, while what distresses us in our individual condition cannot. The contrast is only invalid if nothing in social conditions does deeply distress one. He says of the phrase 'they [scientists] have the future in their bones', both that 'it cannot be explained as a meaningful proposition', and that it dismisses the issue, tacitly eliminates the problem, by implying – I presume this is what Leavis means – that the future will be something to exult in. But surely the phrase means that scientists now habitually deal in kinds of knowledge and power that become socially significant some twenty or fifty years later; so that what is the future for us is contemporary and familiar for them; and that this experience is fundamental in their intellectual life. It does not mean that they rejoice simple-mindedly in the approach of that future. Snow's own warnings about the probability of thermonuclear war surely demonstrate *his* sense of the future.

Snow's style, manner, tone, are indeed 'Wellsian'. As such, of course, they offend against the contemporary intellectual mood. But they are not 'crass', and nothing Leavis has said shows that. We must examine Snow's propositions with an open mind, not predisposed to find them invalid.

When we come to consider those propositions, the ideas of *The Two Cultures*, we must grant Leavis one important point. Snow dismisses the historical record of 'the literary culture' in England far too cavalierly. This lends substance to Leavis's claim that Snow 'knows nothing of history' or of the meaning of civilization. When Snow says that the traditional literary culture did not notice the Industrial Revolution, or when it did notice, didn't like what it saw, then he does expose himself to the sort of scornful punishment which Leavis is administering. The tradition of culture-criticism, explored by Raymond Williams in *Culture and Society*, is one of the two or three great achievements of modern English thought, and it is predominantly the work of the literary culture. However, Leavis's correctness seems to me in this case a debating triumph; because if you *are* deeply aware of that tradition, you are all the more interested in what Snow has to say. It is precisely in the context of those social insights of Ruskin and Lawrence that the thesis of *The Two Cultures* becomes more than a Sunday-newspaper platitude. The literary culture of the nineteenth and twentieth centuries did think harder and to more purpose than any other group about the human problems created by the Industrial Revolution; and Dr Leavis is the great inheritor of that great tradition; but neither they nor he have been able to 'solve' (analyse satisfyingly) some of those problems, and Snow helps us to understand why. *The Two Cultures* brings new life to that tradition of thought.

Dr Leavis's other critical points are less convincing. He accuses Snow of slipping from one meaning of 'culture' to another unconsciously; of ignoring crucial distinctions. But the cases he cites are all ones where he is imposing his own sense of what the critical distinctions are on the argument – he does not respect Snow's line of thought enough to accord it patient attention. Thus at one point Snow identifies the traditional culture in the nineteenth century with the literary culture; they were often different enough, and from Leavis's point of view, essentially so – the great writers were radical and even revolutionary in their ideas. But if there is anything in Snow's argument at all, there is a sense in which the intellectual content of that traditional culture became more and more literary in its bias, as it became more and more alienated from technological industrialism.

He does not bring up two objections to Snow's use of the word which most literary people raise. Some say that the word can only be used of a society as a whole; others that the intellectual and imaginative habits shared by scientists are not general enough in their implications to deserve the name. But this is, as Leavis implicitly admits, pedantry. There are fifty meanings for the word 'culture'. Snow uses it to mean fragments of a whole-society culture. England has two cultures in the sense that our two main sets of intellectual habits and efforts have so little contact and interaction. This is perfectly clear and straightforward.

Then Leavis dismisses as invalid Snow's parallels between people and achievements in the arts and other people and achievements in the sciences. For instance, Snow compared Rutherford's position in the Thirties with T. S. Eliot's, and some knowledge of the Second Law of Thermodynamics with having read one of Shakespeare's plays. Leavis says flatly that such things are incommensurable, but here again one feels that he has been too impatient with the argument as a whole to adopt the point of view from which such propositions are meaningful. For a great many research students and teachers of the Thirties Rutherford and Eliot must have had parallel positions – and opposite influences; representing to students of English (and all literatures to some extent) and of Physics (and all sciences to some extent) not only great intellectual achievement, but the specifically modern forms of the intellectual life; representing it, moreover, by their personalities, their general attitudes, their lives, as well as by their work. The Second Law of Thermodynamics is a key piece in the jigsaw of modern science, connecting with a dozen branches of knowledge, and in itself a most vivid, even melodramatic, concept; to know of it, once to have undergone its imaginative excitement, *is* similar to having once read *Macbeth*; not to know it is as clear a signal as not having read *Macbeth* that enormous areas of thought and imagination are cut off from one's understanding.

Finally, he accuses Snow of being simple-minded in his use of words like 'belief', but here his argument recoils on itself. Snow said that statistically speaking more scientists are unbelievers than believers, in religious terms, and more are on the Left than on the Right, politically. Leavis pours scorn on such simplifications as blurring all the important distinctions, but it is his own recourse to complexities that strikes the reader as the more naïve of the two. Snow's definitions are adequate to his argument at that point. To reject them means that you dismiss that kind of definition always. Leavis, one is bound to suspect, is never interested in whether a man votes Labour or Conservative, whether or not he subscribes to a creed. In a novel, it is true, such categories may be so loose as not to tell you much about a character's intellectual life; but in effective social thinking they remain indispensable.

Social thinking, however, Leavis treats as something which is outside culture itself, and to which culture owes a quite single duty of restraint. Great literature, he tells us, asks deeply important questions about the civilization around it, but 'of course, to such questions there can't be, in any ordinary sense of the word, answers.' Its questions, moreover, will all be of the sort to make society hesitate, slow down, lose confidence in the future, distrust both social planning and technological advance. Any vigorous hope, any eager use of the new powers, will have to come from outside 'culture'. Asking such questions, and allowing no 'ordinary' answers, literature's contribution to social thought is going to be very lop-sided. But with this we begin to enumerate the ways in which the Richmond Lecture offers evidence for Snow's thesis.

The remarkable unanimity of the British literary world against Snow simply expresses, of course, a vested-interest anger. Its members have felt themselves criticized. The scientific world has not rallied to his defence because of a more complicated snobbery. Snow's admirers have been among editors, administrators, vice-chancellors, and the intellectual front-line naturally resents (with about as much justification as front-line troops resent their staff-officers) the large-toned comments of people from outside, and (administratively) above. And this initial resentment found an intellectual framework to grow along in the contemporary taste for pure knowledge, the distrust of popularization, the general reaction against encyclopaedism. But there is no more reason to respect these unanimities than those of any other private group when it is criticized from outside. The fundamental issue is something more serious than that.

The fundamental issue is the future of the idea 'culture'. This enormously ramified and tentacular concept, developed, worked on, contributed to, by all the greatest English writers from Coleridge and Burke to Lawrence and Eliot, commands great intellectual and practical loyalties in England today. It is a powerful ideal; and among the sets of dedicated people serving and directing it, Dr Leavis and his various disciples are pre-eminent. Culture, according to their understanding, is a set of standards, both intellectually and morally rigorous, and socially very conscientious; but socially it is also completely on the defensive; against the influences of mechanization, mass production, mass media, but also, implicitly, against modern science and technology themselves.

There is plenty of evidence of that defensiveness in the Richmond Lecture. Dr Leavis assures us that he is not a Luddite, but his tone then is so mild as to be vacuous beside his tone when he attacks those who are in any way excited about science or the future. His not being a Luddite is a negation; at best a refusal to join his friends who *are* actively fighting machines; at worst, one suspects, a refusal to accept the theoretical implications of his practical preferences. The only time he confronts Snow's claims for the imaginative and intellectual excitement of science – 'the intellectual depth, complexity, and articulation' – he swerves away into personal satire. He offers no answer to the challenge, and the irrelevance of his sneer at Snow at that point perhaps indicates some embarrassment before it. He goes on to insist that there is a 'prior' human achievement to consider, the creation of 'the human world', in language and literature. This priority, we gather, is not so much in time as in value, and is so overwhelming as quite to dispose of the other's claims to consideration. He talks at length of the 'third realm' to which all that makes us human belongs; which is midway between the merely subjective and fanciful and the purely objective and material.

Now, Dr Leavis never, of course, attacks science as such – his strategy is to cut Snow off from every such sizeable ally – but I think an underlying hostility to it becomes evident when we examine this concept of a third realm. Literature obviously belongs to that realm, as Dr Leavis claims, but what about science? He does not mention that, and though it is clear to any unprejudiced observer that science is just as essentially conceptual and co-operative, is just as pre-eminently a structure of human meaning, there is every reason to doubt whether he would include it. The whole concept of a third realm is introduced to distinguish literature, to give it a pre-eminence, if not a unique position. And note that the purely objective category includes all 'that can be brought into the laboratory and pointed to'. There is every hint that for Dr Leavis, when he is off-guard, at least, even mathematics and physics are merely matters of counting, measuring, and weighing. He makes no mention of those components that make them just as finely and poignantly as literature typical of that third realm. He says that Snow does not 'know what literature is'. The Richmond Lecture offers no evidence that Leavis 'knows what science is', much less that he has enough imaginative experience of it to qualify, enrich, mature, validate, his sharp distrust. He speaks of 'that collaborative human creativity of which literature is the type'. Science is not mentioned. And if literature is *the* type of collaborative human creativity, science – being by any definition opposite in half its features – must indeed seem an inferior, ineffective, unstimulating version. I suggest that science must fill some such humble, ancillary role in Leavis's imagination – when it does not figure as the moloch of machinery or an intellectual slave-labour camp. For if science is to have any dignity, any personality for one, any value beyond the materialistic, instrumental, at best purely logical, then one's idea of culture, of the third realm, of human creativity, must be something of which science also can be a type.

And the consequence of that implicit rejection of science in Leavis is just what Snow remarked in literary men in general; an alienation from the essential conditions of modern society. How could it be otherwise, when what is modern and challenging and painful about the present and future is so intimately associated with science, while the humanities deal so much with the past? We have already seen evidence of this alienation in Leavis's account of culture's duty to modern social thought. And compare his tone about modern America with his tone about the Bushmen; about the former, 'the energy, the triumphant technology, the productivity, the high standard of living, and the life-impoverishment – the human emptiness; emptiness and boredom craving alcohol – of one kind or another'; about the latter, 'those poignantly surviving, primitive people, with their marvellous arts and skills and vital intelligence'. The same thing is implicit in his tone wherever he discusses politics or the use of power in society. An interest in the corridors of power, and for that matter membership of the Athenaeum, are each for him quite simply a condemnation. He identifies Snow with Macmillan, in a moral realm beneath the level of polite discussion, and then throws in all the intellectual weeklies for good measure; all belong to a world 'in which standard of living is the ultimate criterion'. He thinks Snow dismissed as Luddites everyone who talks in *any* other terms than 'productivity' and 'technological progress'. All this surely reveals an extraordinarily, a fantastically fierce distrust of material and social power. He quotes as typical of the truly literary and cultured attitude to social problems, Birkin's speech from *Women In Love*,

'I want every man to have his share in the world's goods, so that I am rid of his importunity, so that I can tell him: "Now, you've got what you want – you've got your fair share of the world's gear. Now, you one-mouthed fool, mind yourself and don't obstruct me." ' There is plenty of reason to agree that this is a typically literary attitude – just as we agree that it is admirable in its place in the novel – but we cannot accept it as adequately representing culture, when it so denudes of all dignity those processes of social life which we cannot conduct successfully if we don't feel them to be important as well as necessary. We shall need our full humanity, as Leavis says, to meet the sharp challenges of the future. But full humanity cannot be guaranteed by a literary sensibility so sharply distinct from and distrustful of other kinds of intellectual and practical experience.

What Snow has to offer the idea of culture is a hint towards a redefinition. That idea has now reached a crucial point in its career, at which its critical powers are very sharp, and its self-confidence perfect, but its posture is completely backward-looking. It is not developing generously. If it can be redefined to include scientific virtues and scientific experience, without losing the sharpness of vision and muscularity of grasp which it has had under Dr Leavis's direction, then it will also be able to address itself to contemporary social facts with new energy, and its future career can be as successful as its past.

This essay by Leavis, and the one I am about to mention, seemed worth answering because they were by such distinguished men, and because they took the subject so seriously, but also because, despite this, they betrayed some irrational, uncontrolled, blinded reactions. The personalness of the remarks about Snow, for instance; the irrelevant attack on him as a novelist; the failure to reply to his argument; the refusal to use, not only his terms, but any comparable or related vocabulary. It seems to me that these essays over and over again justified his criticism, and even exemplify his analysis of the culture they represented. Had the leading literary men been able to reply without these failures of control (palpable, I would say, gross) then his case would have been much weaker than it is. It would have remained self-consistent and undeniable, but its urgency, its relevance, its impact, would have been hypothetical. These counter-attacks betray, don't they, the disturbance caused by a valid criticism?

The chorus of imitation that accompanied them betrayed nothing, but exemplified some of the worst traits of the intellectual life. No one nowadays can write an essay on a related subject, or even an introduction to somebody else's essay, without some hasty reassurance of his superiority to the vulgar outcry. 'To say this is not to share in the popular enthusiasm for C. P. Snow's thesis of the two cultures'; in the tone of Petronius scanning the cheaper seats in the Colosseum from the back of the imperial box. The popular – not to say vulgar – enthusiasm I have seen has been on the part of people trying to get into the box with Petronius. It is surely ironical that the Richmond Lecture should have been the occasion for so many people to come round to an enthusiasm for Dr Leavis; for old literary enemies like Kingsley Amis to accept him at last as their champion; for his controversial manner to be explained, justified, protected, even in the Daily Express. *The vulgarity of joining in the movement, of being on the right side, belonged much more to his supporters in that debate. It became a test of one's intellectual modishness strictly comparable with* Last Year at Marienbad, *or with those coterie enthusiasms – for Auden in the Thirties, let's say – which Dr Leavis has so often excoriated. Fledgeling readers found themselves for once sure of their standards, and sallied forth with maiden insights – 'That Lewis Eliot is nothing like Conrad's Marlow'; and their seniors did little better. Nothing is more disheartening, more damaging to one's sense of vocation, than to observe one's colleagues engage in a conspiracy to suspend the laws of debate, the rules of relevance and logic and attentiveness, and to welcome any mode of attack on a chosen victim. And lamentable is the only word for the spectacle of one's teachers, the men one has chosen to form and mould one's own mind, refusing to listen to reason, unable to reply in kind. The standards invoked in the Richmond Lecture to dismiss Snow – as scientist, as stylist, as thinker – were of a bewildering variety and oddity. There is an almost whining sound in the phrase 'this ancient university' (and 'he is, after all, a Cambridge man') in the mouth of Dr Leavis.*

I should like to give the reader, if I can, some sense of how Snow's arguments worked in my mind, and gathered substance, even while I was concentrating on the purely internal logic of Leavis's and Trilling's answers to him. It became clear, for instance, that they were unwilling to discuss whole orders of fact to which he was pointing; and that this will to ignore was an unusually clear manifestation of the intellectual blindness he alleged. This led one to see that it was precisely that movement in modern literature which Leavis and Trilling represent which best bears out Snow's analysis – that many of the exceptions, the anomalies, the unsatisfactorinesses, in his theory, could be disposed of by concentrating attention on that movement.

The sharpest reactions against The Two Cultures *have all come from representatives of the modern or modernist movement in literature (which is discussed at length later in the book). F. R. Leavis and Lionel Trilling are not only brilliant critics of modern literature, but modern critics. They are members of an intelligentsia, that is, people whose intellectual activity is inseparable from a more general, spiritual, uneasiness with the social status quo, a mission to resist and attack society quite radically. They both, in different ways, disclaim the cruder forms of rebellion, but those disclaimers only bring out the essential, involuntary dissent. The only other contemporary critic of comparable stature, Edmund Wilson, has not, so far as I know, written at length on the two cultures, and this was to be expected. It is not his quarrel; like Snow himself, Wilson is not personally a modern literary figure. Though a brilliant critic of modern writers, he is not in this sense a modern critic. The modern movement in the arts has produced a narrow and intense temper, spiritual as well as intellectual. Like Snow, Wilson gives an impression of broad-based worldliness, of a breadth of satisfactions as well as interests, of being less dependent than Trilling or Leavis on exclusively profound or intense truths. The trenchant common sense of his style contrasts with their more complicated and exalted eloquence.*

It is important to keep this distinction in mind, because it clears up one or two of the confusions that close in as soon as one begins to discuss this problem. What I say about 'the literary mind' or 'the literary intellectual' applies fully only to modern writers and critics. When an opponent points to a professor of English or a contemporary novelist to whom none of these generalizations apply, the explanation is usually that he or she is not modern in his sense.

Obviously, a scholar who spends his time on intellectual history, or on editing seventeenth-century drama, is not likely to feel the kind of scornful hostility to science and industry Snow describes; he will feel only the mild dismay everyone feels, in perhaps a scholarly-cranky way. And the professional popular novelist is likely to accept the rewards of a mechanical civilization as eagerly as any other successful man. The popular novel has never followed the serious novel in emptying itself of content; it is still likely to contain considerable sociological, political, or even industrial-scientific observation. And then there are, of course, several real exceptions even among modern writers, some important. By what right then, it may be asked, do I reserve the terms modern and literary for the people who fit my analysis? By the right that they are the most *important individuals, and have the most important influence, in the whole field. Without Pound and Eliot in Poetry, without Proust, Kafka, Joyce, Dostoevsky, without Leavis and Trilling in criticism, modern literature would not be what it is.*

There are intelligent men writing in each of those genres, who are not notably modern in temperament; and whose reactions to The Two Cultures *are therefore more temperate, more reasonable, more relevant, than those I examine. But those men would nearly all acknowledge a large debt to Leavis and Trilling, would yield them a primacy as spokesmen for the literary culture. They even, most of them, support and argue for the two rebuttals, though at obvious painful cost to their sense of decorum and cogency. Their differentness from Leavis and Trilling in this matter, though it is to be expressed largely as a superiority of understanding and argument, cannot constitute a better title to represent literature as a whole. Theirs are the strengths but also the weaknesses of moderation. To approach the same point from a slightly different angle, though Snow's case applies most damagingly to the modern movement, it is not inapplicable to literary men of other schools and other eras. If they did not in fact suffer from the imbalance he describes, it was because of the* moderation of *their literariness, its alliance to other modes of intelligence in them, their acknowledgement of other criteria — those of common sense, politics, philosophy, religion, etc. That alliance is, of course, the sensible and normal thing, but in modern times some writers have trusted overwhelmingly to their literary intuitions even in non-literary matters. They – when they were also men of first-class intelligence – now represent literature by the special character of their achievement as well as by its magnitude.*

In criticism, for instance, I suggest in my next essay a history of modern literature which would relate it to the history of ideas. I say Lionel Trilling is the man who could write it, and I suggest him because this would have to be a modern history as well as of modern ideas, and something different from what we have had so far. We have had major work in the history of ideas, in modern times. We have The Great Chain of Being. *But Professor Lovejoy's work is out of sympathy with modern criticism, not only in its subject-matter, but in its essential method, as this quotation suggests.*

Most teachers of literature would perhaps readily enough admit that it is to be *studied* – I by no means say, can only be enjoyed – chiefly for its thought-content. . . . And the ideas in serious reflective literature are, of course, in great part philosophical ideas in dilution.

This is a radical dissent from the creed of the modern movement in criticism. Dr Leavis's life-work has been to show us how literature can be studied not for its content but for itself, and that there are such things as literary ideas which are not philosophical ideas in dilution. (So sharp has he made the distinction, so high has he lifted our pride, some now fall into the opposite heresy, and think philosophy deals with literary ideas in dehydration.) One would not expect the two cultures quarrel to seem a very urgent one – a personally urgent one – to Professor Lovejoy. He is a scholar, who acknowledges a kinship to scholars in every other branch of learning, and even a physicist, if he took an interest in the history of his subject, could feel him a colleague. But we have critics as well as scholars in literary studies today (the opposition is unfair to both, of course, but I think it indicates briefly which groups I am referring to) and they are the ones most likely to be concerned with modern literature. It is to them that Snow's analysis applies; in them you are likely to find the really striking ignorance of scientific things, the violent refusal of any interest, the emotional rejection of the contemporary, the scorn for popular and official interpretations, the feeling that they are preserving the last vestige of cultural tradition against everyone else's attack.

On the whole, as is to be expected, the imaginative writers exemplify this more vividly than the critics, because it is their job to express emotional attitudes to the world at large. I discuss later some evidence in the major writers of such rejections of crucial experience. At the other end of the intellectual spectrum we have the social protest of the Beats (not the groups of American poets, but the undifferentiated mass of hangers-on of the arts, in dark glasses and long hair). But for evidence of typical literary attitudes we must turn to the social pronouncements of a middle, more representative category of writer. (It is, of course, significant that the arts should be associated with social rebellion [one cannot imagine the scientific equivalent of Beats] and that society now should include a large segment of such intellectual protesters. But this is a part of the subject which I shall not consider in this book; it is too far towards the sociological end of the spectrum of 'culture'. I want to consider only statements in which the ideas still retain some substance, some integrity, some individuality, and can be examined as significant in their own right, not as mostly symptomatic.)

An obvious place to look for such statements is at a literary conference, at which 'modern' writers tend to predominate, and where they meet as writers and intellectuals, in some sense confronting the non-literary world, issuing communiqués on society and the age. The Congress for Cultural Freedom in Berlin in 1961 seems to have been a good example. The American writers (Mary McCarthy was one) apparently analysed their own society with such bitter and hateful contempt that the African and Asian delegates naturally asked, 'What then has Western culture to offer us? You mean we are better off as we are?' But I have found fuller reports of the 1960 Esquire Literary Conference, where Philip Roth, John Cheever, and James Baldwin, discussed 'Writing in America today'. James Baldwin said, 'There is no structure in American life today and there are no human beings. . . . Somehow the writer must get at the truth buried beneath the surface of American life. I have a vision of truth and goodness beneath the insupportable surface of sleaziness.' He was cheered. John Cheever spoke of 'the abrasive and faulty surface of the United States in the last twenty-five years. . . . Having determined the nightmare symbols of our existence, the characters have become debased and life in the United States in 1960 is Hell . . . the only possible position for a writer now is negation.' At the

*end of the conference someone in the audience pointed out that all the speakers
had presented themselves as victims. Exactly, they replied, delighted, we
are all victims.*

Philip Roth's remarks were later re-presented in an article for Commentary, *where he described how American reality 'defies' the American
writer. 'It stupefies, it sickens, it infuriates.' He declared that he literally
could not believe in Nixon's existence, and quotes other people of literary
sensibility to the same effect. Benjamin de Mott had apparently said in an
earlier issue of the same magazine that the deeply lodged suspicion of the
times in Washington, too, is that contemporary events and individuals are
unreal. The age, he concluded, 'seems at once appalling and ridiculous'.*

*There is surely no need to analyse just what is wrong with these state-
ments. We can all recognize hysteria when we hear it. Nor can we claim
surprise, surely, at finding it there and then. This is what Snow meant by
calling literary people natural Luddites, and in some sense, I claim,
everyone must have known what he meant, and known that he was (to
some degree) right. Leavis and Trilling, however, refused to discuss this
possibility, even as a means to defining its degree, limiting its significance.
They insisted on analysing the motives for saying such things – for seeing
them. It is a classic case of the* argumentum ad hominem *which
returns upon the arguer. For even within their self-chosen limits they failed.
There was no case against Snow. There was one against them.*

Lionel Trilling and the Two Cultures

IN his recent article[1] on the Leavis-Snow controversy, Professor
Trilling has advanced our thinking about the problem in several
ways. His use of the word 'cadres', for instance, illuminates Leavis's
whole career, and makes it usefully parallel with Snow's. Leavis's
writers, critics, teachers of literature, educationists, are to be
found in most universities and literary reviews now, to say nothing
of grammar schools and teachers' training colleges. Snow has not
trained disciples in that sense, but his novels as well as *The Two
Cultures* show his long-term concern to define, to discuss, to publi-
cize, the new class of scientific intellectuals, the young physicists,

[1] *Commentary*, 1961.

chemists, biologists, engineers. And it is on behalf of each of these two groups (this is the special interest of Trilling's observation), on behalf of their conflicting claims to speak for the modern consciousness, the modern mind pondering the world's problems, that the two leaders have clashed so bitterly.

This bitterness (another of Trilling's points) is appropriate to a conflict within the 'cultural mode of thought', which takes a man's style and his tastes as involuntary as well as voluntary evidence of his intelligence and character. 'Culture' predicates connections between many kinds of phenomena (social, intellectual, moral) occurring in an individual or a social group, and so takes one as a sufficient symptom of the whole syndrome. When we participate in this mode of thought we judge a man as a whole by what may seem to him like a non-significant choice or reaction, and even by one he is not conscious of making for himself. No doubt the greatest examples of systems of cultural thought remain Marxism and Freudianism, but, especially in England, the word culture itself has been the focus of a third quite formidable rival.

Trilling claims to see another appropriateness in the triumph of this mode of thought in an age dominated by advertising; because advertising, too, tells us we commit ourselves, define ourselves, *become* ourselves, by choosing this rather than that ostensibly innocent alternative. Here again Trilling helps us recognize our own vaguer restiveness. The idea of culture, in its present form, has become stale. Its application to literature no longer, or rarely now, produces interesting criticism. What to change it for is, of course, a more difficult problem. Trilling offers us the idea of Mind; which includes intellectual work of all kinds, each recognizing its kinship to the other kinds, detached, in intention, from those considerations of time and place which culture regards as esemplastic, and detached, too, from the passions; which are for culture the life-blood of all thought. Such a suggestion can be only, at this stage, a signpost; it tells us very little more about the Promised Land than the direction in which it lies, but that direction is a very attractive one as seen from this particular impasse. That is so not just because of the ugly passions which are being particularly indulged in this cultural debate, but because what is so loudly absent from the arguments of most of the combatants is any understanding of the intellectual activity the opposite side stands for. Not that either explicitly denies the value of the other's work, but they remove it to a remoteness, an antithesis to their own kind – the kind they *do* understand – so that it becomes effectively unreal. The best efforts towards 'bridging the gap' (and even Dr Leavis admits it exists – he only repudiates all responsibility for it – *they* must cross it to *him*) seem to me those of Stephen Toulmin and June Goodfield, who are writing a history of the sciences which reintegrates them into the general intellectual tradition of the West (a phrase which I take to describe, from an historical point of view, what Trilling describes, from his more dialectical point of view, as Mind). If someone could do the same for the history of literature, without sacrificing that crucial critical autonomy which Dr Leavis has won for us, we would be well advanced towards one culture instead of two, and towards the rejuvenation of culture itself. And when we ask ourselves who might be able to do that for literature, the person we think of is Professor Trilling himself.

In all these ways, therefore, his essay is very helpful. But it makes other points with which it is impossible to agree.

In several places it misrepresents Snow's argument. For instance, it quotes Snow as saying that the existing pattern of traditional culture must be broken if we are to have a tolerable future. But the pattern Snow says must be broken is that of British education, embodying the rigid division between the two cultures in Britain; a much more limited and plausible statement. It says that Snow uses 'literary' and 'traditional' interchangeably; and that if we accordingly transpose them, we find Snow saying that the Western world is still managed by a literary culture; which it interprets further to mean (except that such a statement is obviously meaningless) that such things as the movement of armies and fleets are in the charge of literary men, or men with primarily literary training. This is certainly absurd enough. But in fact 'literary' and 'traditional', in Snow's usage, cover some areas of meaning identically, but not all; 'traditional' includes far more, for one thing; they cannot be interchanged in this instance, but there is no reason why they should be. And the statement judged so meaningless (replacing now the word 'traditional') therefore has its (very striking) reference – to such facts as that the Senior Civil Service has its intellectual training so much in the form of classics at Oxford or Cambridge.[1] Then it represents Snow as *really* saying (implying) that the future (which scientists but not literary men 'have in their bones') is necessarily good; that to entertain the idea that the future might be bad is tantamount to moral ill-will. It claims to be 'astonished' at this idea; but how much more astonished Snow must be, since *The Two Cultures* follows that phrase, 'have the future in their bones', with 'They may or may not like it, but they have it. That was as true of the conservatives J. J. Thomson and Lindemann as of the radicals Einstein or Blackett. . . .' Do any of those names – since Snow's *statements* seem to be dismissed from consideration – do they suggest any confident rush forward into any kind of future, much less the future of the Sixties?

There are several such particular misrepresentations or mis-interpretations, which one gradually realizes are the fruit of, or the justification for, one enormous interpretation. Trilling is dismissing Snow's own statements of his purposes, and sympathies, and general attitudes, in favour of a 'detected' preoccupation and 'unconscious' drive. What Snow is *really* saying, though he nowhere says it, and probably doesn't even realize he means it, is that Russia and the West must come to some sort of mutual understanding, and the way for them to do this is to bring their scientists together, because they all speak the same international language; and to dismiss the literary men, because literature creates differences between classes and nations, is indifferent to human inequality and suffering, and asks 'rude and impertinent questions about the future'. The trouble with this argument, the essay continues (with some odd stylistic echoes of the Richmond Lecture), is that it forgets about politics. 'And it can be said of

---

[1] To quote precise figures, taken from Anthony Sampson's *Anatomy of Britain*, 53 per cent of the new recruits to the Administrative Grade between 1948 and 1956 had studied classics or history, while only 1 per cent had studied any kind of science; and 50 per cent of all recruits were from Oxford, and 30 per cent from Cambridge.

The Two Cultures that it communicates the strongest possible wish that we should forget about politics.' I should say immediately that I see no scrap of evidence for this statement; and as for 'the strongest possible wish that we should forget about politics', I think most people would agree that there is at least one such wish considerably stronger – that communicated by the Richmond Lecture.

Now this need not disconcert Professor Trilling, for he claims that it is the cultural mode, in which Snow and Leavis equally participate, which is responsible for this denial of politics. He should be disconcerted, however, by his own treatment of Snow's argument, which could not be more 'cultural' in this sense; he has ignored the rational, intended meaning of the book, and read enormous (and illusory) things into its style and method. It is surely the teachings of Mind which make us feel that he should have paid more attention to what Snow said he was saying. Mind teaches us that culture's essential weakness is its ambition always to interpret, to look for the non-rational meanings (good or bad) without first asking if the offered argument betrays any significant influence by them. There is, I submit, no reason at all, and therefore no justification, for looking below the surface of any document so simple, clear, and self-consistent as *The Two Cultures*. You have no right to ask what does he really mean when there is no evidence that he does not mean what he says.

The essay goes on to claim that Snow 'says' both that politics cannot be judged (because they do not exist) and that they should not be judged (because the traditional agency of criticism is now irresponsible). This agency is literature, and its irresponsibility, in Snow's eyes, is its function as a criticism of life. Snow wants science and scientist to go their way without any criticism; literature is no longer to be society's loyal opposition; he sees it as a threat to the national well-being. About *1984*, for instance, Snow says that Orwell 'wants the future not to happen'; but this (says Trilling) is like saying that intelligence itself wants the future not to happen.

By this point it is time for the reader to be as astonished at Trilling as he claims to be at Snow. What possible ground can there be (especially from Trilling's point of view) for calling literature *the* traditional agency of criticism of politics? What happened to journalism, history, political theory, etc.? And how can anyone call the Orwell of *1984 the* protagonist of modern intelligence? And who but Trilling himself has shown us that contemporary literature is the most *dis*loyal opposition imaginable, disloyal not just to science and the future, but to every stable and organized social undertaking, to society itself.

Let me quote a passage from his fine essay on 'The Modern Element in Modern Literature'.

The author of *The Magic Mountain* once said that all his work could be understood as an effort to free himself from the middle class, and this, of course, will serve to describe the chief intention of all modern literature. And the means of freedom which Mann prescribes (the characteristic irony notwithstanding) is the means of freedom which in effect all of modern literature prescribes. It is, in the words of Clavdia Chauchat, '*se perdre et même . . . se laisser dépérir*', and thus to name the means is to make plain that the end is not merely freedom from the middle class but freedom from society itself. I venture to say that the idea of losing oneself up to the point of self-destruction, of surrendering oneself to experience without regard to self-interest or conventional morality, of escaping wholly from the societal bonds, is an 'element' somewhere in the mind of every modern person who dares to think of what Arnold in his unaffected Victorian way called 'the fullness of spiritual perfection'.

How can you reconcile this with saying that modern literature is a loyal opposition to society, or a criticism of life in any Arnoldian sense, or merely asks 'rude and impertinent' questions about the future? You cannot. Modern literature does not question, it attacks; and with fury; and not a possible future, but the essential present.

Arnold's historic sense presented to his mind the long, bitter bloody past of Europe, and he seized passionately upon the hope of true civilization at last achieved. But the historic sense of our literature has in mind a long excess of civilization to which it ascribes the bitterness and blood of both the past and the present and of which it conceives the peaceful aspects to be mainly contemptible – its order achieved at the cost of extravagant personal repression, either that of coercion or that of acquiescence; its repose otiose; its tolerance either flaccid or capricious; its material comfort corrupt and corrupting; its taste a manifestation either of timidity or of pride; its rationality attained only at the price of energy and passion.

How can you reconcile this with saying, apropos of Snow, that
we must try to understand

what this passionate hostility to society implies, to ask whether it is a symptom,
sufficiently gross, of the decline of the West, or whether it is not perhaps an
act of critical energy on the part of the West, an act of critical energy on the
part of society itself – the effort of society to identify in itself that which is but
speciously good, the effort to understand afresh the nature of the life it is designed to foster. I would not anticipate the answer, but these questions make,
I am sure, the right way to come at the phenomenon.

You cannot reconcile them. Modern literature, as Trilling has
amply demonstrated, does *not* try to identify that which is but
speciously good, it attacks the genuinely good in society as well, it
attacks the life of society. Those last sentences are deeply unsatisfactory. It is disingenuous to say he has not anticipated the
answers to his questions. It is disingenuous to call them questions
at all, since they are so carefully phrased to exclude the answer no.
And yet, so profound is his ambivalence that, in another place,
and with far more conviction and cogency, he himself has given
exactly that answer.

There is far more reason to interpret, to talk of unconscious
intentions, with this essay than with Snow's. Besides the inconsis-
tencies between this and the earlier better statement, there are
tortuous waverings and tenuosities within the argument itself. The
advocate of modern literary training is *not*, we are told, defending
the indefensible. He can make clear that literature's social value
quite straightforwardly.

The advocacy can be conducted in honest and simple ways. It is not one of
those ways to say that literature is by its nature or by definition innocent – it is
powerful enough to suppose that it has the possibility of doing harm. But the
ideational influence of literature is by no means always as direct as, for polemi-
cal purposes, people sometimes say it is.

Whether or not this is honest, no one could call it simple. And as
for the honesty, is it not so circumlocutory just because, bluntly
put, this idea undercuts the previous claim of 'powerfulness' for
literature? Has literature, or has it not, 'the possibility of doing
harm'? One wants to ask that also because elsewhere (in the essay

on 'Modern Literature' again) Trilling himself has asserted, has demonstrated, the ideological *effectiveness* of art in modern society. Let me quote two more sentences from the essay.

And in this connection the teacher will have in mind the peculiar prestige that our culture, in its upper reaches, gives to art, and to the ideas that art proposes – the agreement, ever growing in assertiveness, that art yields more truth than any other intellectual activity. . . . For many students no ideas that they will encounter in any college discipline will equal in force and sanction the ideas conveyed to them by modern literature.

In this new essay he tries to deny that force and sanction, to so circumscribe them as to effectively exculpate art, but his own words offer the logical objection.

Every university teacher of literature will have observed the circumstance that young people who are of radical social and political opinion are virtually never troubled by the opposed views or the settled indifference of the great modern writer. . . . I have yet to meet the student committed to an altruistic politics who is alienated from Stephen Dedalus by that young man's disgust with political idealism, just as I have yet to meet the student from the most disadvantaged background who feels debarred from what Yeats can give him by the poet's slurs upon shopkeepers or by anything else in his inexhaustible fund of snobbery.

No, they are not troubled, because they perceive that they are on the same side after all – against society. That, as Trilling himself has pointed out, is the crucial battle; one can welcome the co-operation of Joyce and Yeats, and Lawrence and Kafka and Proust, however democratic one's own politics, when one's deeper aim is 'to cut oneself off from the middle class'. We cannot accept any such evidence that students of modern literature are self-insulated against its ideological effect. And indeed the analysis of that insulation is quite unconvincing.

They perceive that the tale is always on the side of their own generous impulses. They know that, if the future is in the bones of anyone, it is in the bones of the literary genius, and exactly because the present is in his bones, exactly because the past is in his bones. They know that if a work of literature has any true artistic existence, it has value as a criticism of life; in whatever complex way it has chosen to speak, it is making a declaration about the qualities that life should have, about the qualities life does not have but should have. They feel, I think, that it is simply not possible for a work of literature that comes within the borders of greatness *not* to ask for more energy and fineness of life, and, by its own communication of awareness, bring these qualities into being.

This is what rationalist writers used to call mysticism. 'They perceive that . . . they feel that . . . it is simply not possible that . . .' The emphasis is urgent and repetitive. The writer is trying to convince himself by rhetoric, because the rational content of his argument is inadequate. Of course modern literature creates energy and fineness of life; but there is no guarantee that those kinds may not be hostile to others. Surely a literary education yields among its first-fruits the sophisticated awareness of good things that cost terribly, some that cost too much, in the way of other good things? Isn't this the kind of mistake a scientific education might conceivably leave one vulnerable to, but that *we* are professionally protected against? The energy Lawrence and Kafka and Joyce and Proust bring us is very hard to reconcile with social participation. Consequently, a literary education is a dangerous preparation for social and political responsibility. These surely are facts. Heaven knows they are not the only relevant ones. But they are important and they must be faced. These are not things Snow said. They are things Trilling himself said on another occasion, and his denial of them here is not only unconvincing and irrelevant; it is a symptom, I would claim, of some panic. The engineer is shouting the praises of a structure whose weaknesses he himself fears because he knows them better than the enemy does.

Finally, let us consider what the essay has to say about the place of science in general education.

Snow fears literature's function as the criticism of life, we are told, and criticism's concern to see the object as in itself it really is. These are essential aims of all education, and it is because Snow fears them that he does not make a single substantive proposal about education. And at the beginning of the essay, Arnold is quoted again, with approval, to the effect that science does not serve the instinct for conduct or the instinct for beauty, but culture does; culture here being defined to comprise all the humane intellectual disciplines.

The trick here, as in so many of these arguments, is that science is so smoothly defined as a non-humane intellectual discipline. From then on, of course, there can be no dissent. It is much as if history were defined as a non-speculative accumulation of facts, and then argued to be not an art. Or as if literature were denied the right to include historical and philosophical considerations in its judgements, and then argued to be narrow. It is true that science has been and is taught in a non-humane way, but that does not define its nature once for all. The poor teaching of science is a well-publicized problem, and there are many 'substantive proposals' for solving it in circulation. In America there is the system of repeating famous experiments of the past, described by Conant and practised at the University of Chicago; and the Harvard course devised by Gerald Holton, which emphasizes the general ideas implicit in particular scientific procedures.[1] What much more needs saying nowadays is not how to make training in science broader but how to make training in literature narrower, more logically stringent. There is much more humility and realism about their educational problems among scientists than among humanists. Literary students must be made to see that they are not merely acquiring taste, but reasoning. Of course, such reasoning consists largely of acts of recognition and response which are difficult to break down into a series of steps, difficult above all to repeat with new material, to apply formally and prescriptively. Nevertheless, we do know, after the fact, why and how we arrived at a particular judgement, and that knowing why is a part of the study of literature. That study should be so performed as to dramatize its qualities of exactness, and logic, and demonstration. It is too easy to get through literature examinations by mere sensitiveness, just as it is by mere mechanicalness in science examinations. Science is perhaps in worse case, but the important point is that both sides need to move towards a middle mode, a more generally intellectual mode.

I don't mean to deny the existence of the problem, but to assert the existence of solutions – of substantive proposals for the humanization of scientific education. Science could become a humane intellectual discipline tomorrow; that is, in as short a

[1] I deal with several other such ideas in detail in Chapter 6 of this book.

time as is needed to train humane teachers and institute humane syllabuses. What prevents that from happening is the effective disbelief of many who say of course science is a part of culture, and the effective hostility of many who say of course *science* is all right, but technology, or scientism, or applied science, is a totally different matter. This seems to me to justify the way Snow chose to attack the problem; from on top, so to speak; predicating (though politely) concealed prejudices which obstruct progress most people have theoretically agreed on. The fuss and fury he stirred up certainly demonstrated those prejudices; I think it reasonable to claim they demonstrated fear and guilt, too.

In the mind of the humane scientist, science is already a part of culture, and the Arnoldian antithesis collapses. Humanely taught, science trains the mind, 'prepares one for life', as fully as literature. Not that it can ever, I imagine, serve the instinct for conduct as fully as literature; because the whole world of personal relations bulks so large in conduct; but on the other hand, the instinct for truth is probably better served (better satisfied, disciplined, toughened) by science. Above all, this kind of competitiveness becomes childish once we learn how to recognize both as modes of Mind, once we teach both as parallel branches of the Western intellectual tradition.

Professor Trilling's essay seems to me an even more poignant proof than the Richmond Lecture (because more considered and superficially calm) of the panic into which Snow's simple and moderate statements of obvious truths have flung even the very best representatives of literature. And this panic begins to cast a lurid light of significance back on those statements.

Thinking about the Trilling essay – its differences from as well as its likenesses to the Leavis essay – also led me to another important clue to unravel part of the problem.

The argument over culture is after all a peculiarly British one, and I sometimes thought even Professor Trilling showed some misapprehension of what Dr Leavis, and the others, got so heated about. He described it, for instance, as a revival of the Huxley-Arnold debate; but the word 'culture' has acquired a more strongly anthropological meaning since then. Also this quarrel is in no significant sense a revival. It has a long history, but the relevance of the feelings aroused is ultimately as well as immediately to contemporary facts; to the modern movement in literature, for instance, which, as Trilling himself says, means something so different now from what it meant in Arnold's day.

The word culture has come to mean more in modern England than anywhere else, I reflected. In the West as a whole it has seemed hopeless in this century to demand a complete scheme of knowledge from an educated man; not only because modern knowledge is vast, but because so much of it has seemed merely technical. At the same time, culture, which is dependent on general knowledge, has come to seem more and more the guardian of all that is best in society. Consequently one branch of knowledge, literature, has extended its purview more and more, and arrogated to itself more and more of the duties of general humanistic culture. This happened in England more than anywhere else because modern literature was represented by two great figures, a novelist and a critic, who peculiarly concerned themselves with the country's culture as a whole. These two, D. H. Lawrence, and F. R. Leavis, reacted against the anti-humanism, the social disengagement, of modern literature, by inventing for themselves a putative society to which they (though perhaps nobody else) could sincerely belong. (Leavis's 'Cambridge despite Cambridge'.) What people mean by culture in England is thus a very explosive combination of social disgust and social enthusiasm, and their own recipe for it is both a very private possession and a very general truth; one by which they define themselves in opposition to the rest of the world, and one which they think defines their mode of positive relationship to the rest of the world.

This has not, I realized, happened so much in America, and the word culture is a less exciting one at high levels of discourse there. Perhaps the concept 'America' has shared with 'culture' the equivalent loyalties there. The American experience, the American dream, the American failure, the American guilt, these are key ideas in terms of which people define themselves and their society. In their use you find the same hypertrophy of literary insights as in England you find in theories of culture. Perhaps Americans should imagine they are defining 'America' as well as 'culture' if they are to understand our passionateness. Certainly, I thought, we must realize how many conflicting and enormous ideas we are packing into one word.

2. Two defences of my own project

I

My 'project' was simply to acquire some knowledge of science, some minimal scientific education, in the hope I could thus throw off the handicaps, the lop-sided development, that resulted from a too literary training.

The next two essays are two talks I gave for the BBC during my year at Cambridge; and deal with some difficulties arising early in the attempt. The first reflects one of the simplest but most nagging problems in any project of re-education, one's fear that what one is working on is 'not the real thing'. There are plenty of people to tell you that you are only learning your alphabet in physics, and that your textbook exercises have no more in common with a real scientist's work than the Russian alphabet, or perhaps Russian grammar, has with War and Peace. *I am fairly sure now that that is not true, but it did seem plausible. I had to work out, to my own satisfaction, the relationships and different validities of different kinds of scientific knowledge; I had to know what was the correct analogy for my kind of scientific knowledge in relation to that of the real scientist.*

The second talk reflects my attempts to answer a different kind of questioning. 'What good do you think this will do?' and 'Do you think all of us so narrow?' And 'Why don't you learn something about your own subject first?'

The talk on popularization set out only to express my indignation at prejudices that seemed like extraneous and accidental obstacles in my bath. But I soon saw that they were not accidental; they were another face of that aggressive provincialism, that intellectual lop-sidedness, I was trying to correct in myself – more exactly, those general prejudices are specially strong nowadays because that lop-sidedness, in others as well as in myself, is specially developed. People despise popularization because they disbelieve in all attempts at a broader culture.

Popularization

THIS word, popularization, is one of that kind that do unintentional harm even in their most innocuous uses. It is one of the prime agents in that conspiracy we call the two cultures, a conspiracy to divide and enfeeble the modern mind. Because it implies that the thing popularized has been reduced in value, and that the people reading it have been fobbed off with a substitute. It divides by implying that modern science, for instance, is so remote from the literary man's understanding that his idea of it is only half true. And it enfeebles by implying that the only things we really know are a handful of specialties (if we are lucky enough to be specialists in something) and that the rest of our intellectual life is a game of blind man's buff.

This is done typically at the universities, to impressionable, eighteen-year-old minds. The word is one you hear often at lectures and tutorials and undergraduate discussions. The lecturer says, 'This idea has, of course, been the subject of a certain amount of popularization', and a ripple of sympathetic disgust passes over the upturned faces. Or he says, 'Despite what you may have read in the Sunday newspapers on this subject', and a titter runs round the room. Or, at the end of the hour, he says, 'Of course, this has been a very superficial and popularized treatment of the problem, but it's all we have time for'; and as the students gather up their books, the honest ones add to themselves, 'It's all I'll ever have time for', and gradually the conviction accumulates that they don't know anything as it should be known, even in their own subject.

This is true for all areas of knowledge. A popular history of literature is thought to be an undignified way for even a science undergraduate to find out about poetry, and any reading of popularized science I did while I was studying English seemed to me like reciting 'A is for apple'. It didn't occur to me that I was, though in an elementary way, getting at important truths.

Popularization is, then, a word with a moral identity. It refers ostensibly to the act of making a technical subject understandable to someone not trained in that technique; but it implies, in fact, that the cases it describes are those where the subject is misrepresented by this treatment. Where the truth of the matter has been diluted, if not falsified. Where the result is something you yourself would not read, except with a feeling of being condescended to, and of yourself condescending. But what about those cases where a technically difficult subject has been made clear to the layman without suffering any diminution or dilution or falsification? There is no word for such cases. Some people would say, of course, that there are none – that such a thing can't happen – that truth can only be conveyed in esoteric language which must be specially learned for each new subject. Not everyone believes that, however; some of us believe in several levels of complexity and completeness of statement as all true; but everyone has to *talk* as if the other theory were undeniable. They have to use the word popularization, which implies that.

It has, then, a social effect similar to that Raymond Williams ascribes to the term 'the masses' in *Culture and Society*. He discusses the work that word does on the whole culture in which it is operative, on the society which uses it to describe large groups of its members; even if I personally say 'the masses' without condescending to the people I describe by it, my listener will hear a condescension – and in a sense it is there, in the word. Raymond Williams gives us a whole set of such words, all of which were invented to suit the needs of the Industrial Revolution and the crisis in culture that it provoked. Popularization belongs to that list historically, too. It seems to have been first used around 1836, which is the time 'working classes' and 'industrialism' and 'artistic' were coined.

Of course, there are dozens of examples of popularization which deserve and actively arouse the prejudice the word embodies. The misuse of metaphysics and metaphor in Sir James Jeans's work, and Eddington's, has been sufficiently exposed by Susan Stebbing to stand for the whole category of more pretentious works. Even within the humbler group, concerned more limitedly with scientific *fact*, there is plenty to distrust. I found a highly recommended one recently with examples of all those features that most alienate an educated reader. There were gross factual errors; it said that Tycho Brahe discovered the elliptical motion of the planets, and that the sexuality of plants was not known before the nineteenth century; and the author is a man of science – on his own ground, and when he cares, he can be as accurate as anybody else. Then it was full of those half-truths and vaguenesses (that, for instance, modern science is humble, because it admits the existence of chance) which offend the scrupulous reader more than outright mistakes, because they give that flatulent sensation of (unearned) familiarity with the subject. And thirdly, worst of all, it was full of jazzy, neon-lit allusions to gayer experience which kept nudging the reader's ribs as if he were incapable by himself of sustained attention. It described two galaxies of stars in collision as 'mingling and interweaving like the chorus in a Hollywood musical spectacle'. The writer obviously feared that if he used a more purely explanatory figure, the reader would get bored. He assumed, that is, that you are jigging round the room to the sound of a jukebox while you are reading his book, and that nothing but an appeal to your native tastes can rivet your attention.

That is an example of popularization at its worst, but one cannot say that it is untypical, because the idea of the type is so vague in this genre. There is no serious or stringent idea available of what makes a book a worthy example of popularization. Every aspect of that book tells the reader that its writer is not trying hard and does not respect his own work; and so, if one notices such things, one concludes that popularized science is not written for oneself, but for other stupider people. (That is one reason why people who know how to read are often more ignorant of science than the less fastidious.) The writer may, in fact, be trying very hard in other ways, and may 'believe in' what he is doing. There were some good passages in that book. But it did not occur to the author, apparently, that the lay reader may be someone as intelligent as himself in non-scientific matters, someone with as much taste, tact, and general education as himself. He condescended to his reader, and in that at least he was typical of nearly all his colleagues.

But if a writer is to popularize successfully, he must follow the same rules as for any other kind of good writing – he must imagine a reader like himself, only more intelligent, and with plenty of adult experience, but ignorant of this particular subject. We are all of us laymen in nine-tenths of the subjects we nevertheless need to understand.

And he may then convey the *truth* of his subject. It will not be the version he would offer to fellow specialists, but it will be fully true, if it is a vivid accurate outline of his own more detailed understanding, and if it is intelligently related to the rest of a layman's knowledge. If someone asks me where I live, I can mention the name of the town, or, if the inquirer is a foreigner, I can describe the area of England and the industrial character of the town, or, if he is coming to visit me, I can describe the trains and buses and turnings he needs to know to get there. But I don't feel that even in the first case, if I said no more than 'I live in the heart of Birmingham', I told a half-truth. It gives my inquirer a clear accurate picture, and he can put it together with other facts about me, and with the same fact about other people, and understand the world better. A specialist ought surely often to tell his knowledge in this form, for his own sake. The version he shares with fellow specialists is likely to contain a good many hidden assumptions, if not confusions.

It is obvious that the writers of popularized learning need to believe in this kind of truth-telling. Just because they don't, their work lacks real self-respect, and the self-discipline that would derive from that. It is clear, though less important, that specialists should believe in and practise this secondary way of expounding the truths of their specialty. But is it not just as true that we all need to believe in it, to create that faith as a fact of our corporate consciousness; not just so that those others can believe it, but so that we can all participate fully in our world?

Certainly it is natural that in any educational community like a university there should be sharp and scornful distinctions drawn, between full and three-quarters knowledge. It is not only natural, it is necessary. Moreover, if intellectual life is to maintain its vigour, it must be allowed freedom; freedom to, among other things, withdraw voluntarily from common understanding. We have had great periods of popularization, for instance in the eighteenth century, and so much clarity and publicity of thought made some branches of learning retreat deliberately into obscurity at the end of the century. They could not develop along those lines any longer. It is, in fact, something similar that has happened in this century.

But we must not, therefore, think the specialism of today inevitable or harmless. We should not allow words like popularization to make us despise all broader knowledge. For we live in a state of intellectual crisis or near-crisis; and one quite directly connected with a political crisis which threatens all of us with personal disaster. The intellectual problem is that we are all so shockingly ignorant of at least half of the culture we live in; illiterate rather than ignorant. And the connection of this with the Cold War, and the possibility of real war, is that we hardly know what it is we stand for, fight for, are threatened for. We can recite a political creed, and we can feel, on a more emotional, domestic level, that there are things we would die to defend. But thinking people need to believe (*do* believe, inarticulately and feebly) in something else between those two, something in our society to be both experienced and idealized, and much more analogous to the faith that inspires Communism. A great many thinking people in the West surely lack that faith. They are clear that they don't want Communism; passionate that they personally would not live under it; but far from passionate, not even clear, that our system should triumph, should spread, should grow. Their faith (in all the things we place our faith in) is weak.

Among those things we place our faith in is what we sometimes call freedom of thought; but, in so far as it regards the life of learning, the phrase is dead, because the idea behind it is inarticulate, the experience it reports is unexperienced. Even intellectual people have so little knowledge of that universe of evolving thought that is embodied, in the institutional sense, in the universities of this country, and of America, and of the West generally. It is a universe because it contains so many things, novels and literary criticism and biochemistry and atomic physics and psycho-analysis and linguistics, etc., and of so many different intellectual kinds, inventions and theories and art and research, and yet they all belong together, as the objects of the physical universe do. That universe is alive and growing here just as vigorously, and much more freely, than in Russia and China; much more fully, in the whole area of the arts; and that fact, for all our manifold manifest weaknesses, is a great moral justification. It is perhaps the most splendid single facet, single realization, of this liberty we talk about so vaguely and yet must in some sense believe is there. But this universe, this firmament of thought, is divided up, blocked off from us, by barriers of mutual ignorance. We just don't know, or try to know, about things outside our own specialty. Practically no one is aware of the scope, the power, of that universe, or can take pride in it in the easy natural way that constitutes faith. People know there is development and achievement in their own line, but that is something one takes for granted and privately. It is the element they inhabit, within which they work and breathe. It is only when they travel from one area of thought to another, and participate imaginatively, that they get a feeling of exhilaration and community. That feeling our civilization can still give, and must give if it is to survive. At least if it is to satisfy us, to sustain us in living as we have to live, under the pressures we have to feel.

It would be too big a job to trace the history of this compartmentalization of our minds, and to guess why educated people now so distrust any popularized form of knowledge. But we can point out the great triumphs of pure science and pure art in our century. Meaning by pure both very self-directed and out of relation to any social purpose, and also very abstract and hard for a layman to understand. This pure science, for instance modern theoretical physics, and pure art, for instance James Joyce's novel *Ulysses*, have achieved very exciting and powerful things in our century. Beside them everything else has seemed like a compromise intellectually, or a bit inane. The broader, less pure subjects, like history, have seemed tepid beside them.

So all virtue has been assigned to narrow and intense kinds of knowledge. Even the historians of science, who stand for communication between academic subjects, are patronizing about popularization. They treat it always as a diminution of the truth. Socially, it may sometimes be necessary, and even praiseworthy. Intellectually, it is always somewhat ignominious and comic. In one of the best known of such histories, for instance, the remarks about Fontenelle perfectly catch the tone of this prejudice. It is said that Fontenelle 'made science amusing to fashionable ladies and as easy as the latest novel'. And this is popularization itself which is dismissed, not Fontenelle's performance; for he is at the same time said to be a perfect model for all popularizers after him.

Now, I want science made easy and clear to me, but of course I don't want to think of myself as a fashionable lady, or as one who 'reads the latest novel'. I think of what I'm doing as something strenuous and difficult – quite as effortful as most specialist academic work. But it is hard in the present climate of opinion, under the baleful influence of words like 'popularization', to make other people see it that way, and therefore fully to believe it oneself.

The historian of science referred to there is Herbert Butterfield, in The Origins of Modern Science, *but his remark, his tone, could be paralleled from a dozen others. Most historians make no distinction between popularizing scientific knowledge, and making it readable, or making it fashionable, or making it available to the non-scientifically educated. They lump together everything in the field of non-technical science, and 'fashionable', 'amateur', 'popularized', 'simplified', all have the same flavour of dismissal.*

The book of popularization referred to is Ritchie Calder's Science Makes Sense; *here, too, I could have multiplied my examples a hundredfold; and it is just because the historians, and the science teachers, and the critics and reviewers, make no distinctions within the field, that such mistakes are made so easily. 'Popularization' covers eighteen varieties of presentation and imposes no standards on any of them; writers feel the pressure of no discipline as they write, and excuse themselves easily by saying, 'It's only popularized. It's not for the scholars, who are seriously interested. People aren't going to read it that carefully.'*

Nowadays what is popularized is mostly scientific knowledge, and the fog of prejudice around 'science' doubles that around 'popularization'.

'Science for the layman' is one of the most confusing categories we have, and one of the most confused collections of material. The reader finds his role varying from book to book, and sometimes from page to page, between the babe in arms, who widens his eyes when told that the human body is 70 per cent water, and the lab assistant, who nods briskly when reminded of the Krebs citric acid cycle. And often when the reader is neither confused nor condescended to, he is still not given, what in this dialogue he so much needs, a positive identity. Fred Hoyle's book on the stars is one of the few that does give one a sense of who and what one is, as a layman in science; what kind of responsible relationship one can have to a mass of facts one knows mainly by proxy; how one can be both technically ignorant and imaginatively informed. That book's idea of the layman rather stresses the first part of the word, but it remains a valid idea, to which the reader is ready to assimilate himself. Irving Adler's Stepping Stones to Space tackles more difficult things in astronomy, and explains them equally well. But you don't get from Adler's book that sustaining sense of why you are acquiring these pieces of information rather than any other; how they are nourishing one's total imaginative life, one's power of response to the general world. The reader is given no sense of his identity, and it is therein a less successful piece of science for the layman. There is no centre to it or to most of these books; and that is because there is no centre and no order to their archetype, their category.

One can make some distinctions within the group. There is science for the lay-child; where the pages are peppered with exclamation marks, explicit and implicit; you are in your play-pen being taught to count by a twinkling man with a twinkling stethoscope. There is science for the layman proper; which doesn't necessarily assume that the reader knows anything at all, but allows for the possibility that he may know quite a lot. There is science for the lay-scientist; the latest news from some field of research, translated into the simpler language appropriate to workers in related fields. In this category I would put such magazines as The Scientific American and The New Scientist, not to mention Nature. These terms are perhaps useful mainly to help us dismiss certain illegitimate claims on our attention, to let us concentrate on the category of the layman proper. Within that category we may then need some more divisions. We certainly need the invention of some new terms to help communication – to let the critic or commentator tell the reader just what to expect from a particular *book. Even then, the field must remain various. But this need not make the idea of the reader vague. The situation is only that in imaginative literature. There are hard poems and easy ones, but if you have a taste for poetry you find that even extremes of both kinds are written for you. Exactly the same reader can turn from* The Waste Land *to 'Tiger, tiger'; and the same reader can turn from Morris Kline's* Mathematics in Western Culture *to* Hoyle, *or from Courant and Robbins's* What is Mathematics? *to Kline.*

Since the field is so confused, perhaps differentiations are not so useful as a defining principle. What distinguishes all science for the layman from other kinds of science is the purpose for which it is intended. And this purpose, I would argue, is the discipline of the imagination. In discipline one, of course, includes stimulation, and imagination must be read to include intellectual and moral faculties. These books, that is, aim to tell us about the physical complex in which we live in such detail and such order as to form a satisfying response in us; satisfyingly vivid, sober, strong, integrated. Besides the physical complex (the word Nature no longer seems quite real) they tell us about the great machines and great structures, including the army of men within them, and the fantastic expenditures they involve. And finally they tell us something about science itself, its origins, its essential character, the latest techniques and the new findings.

This is an enormous definition. It is an enormous subject-matter, and one which offers writers fine opportunities. The imagination of the modern intelligentsia, in its most highly developed forms, is unbalanced, misshapen; it is over-literary, too purely psychological-moral; this whole 'natural' mode of experience turns sentimental in its grasp, leaves it merely nostalgic, or bored, or appalled, while still uninformed. Most people who are literarily educated, and perhaps especially those with very active and responsible imaginations, just don't know enough to form an adequate response to half of their environment; the more changing and challenging half. Science for the layman must remedy that ignorance and form those responses.

But enormous though this definition is, it does not include arm-chair textbooks, even with answers at the back; or books of mathematical puzzles (for the fancy rather than the imagination); or sheer collections of information. And it rations the amount of technical apparatus (symbols, formulae, long words) to the minimum that serves the overriding purpose. But it admits no inference that the truth is being watered down; this would perhaps be better called non-technical science than science for the layman, for it claims to be just as scientific, just as true, as the more esoteric kinds.

Science as an imaginative discipline, non-technical science, would have to aim at its own kind of authority; the kind a critical essay can achieve in literary matters, without a formidable array of footnotes or bibliography. On the other hand, it must equally avoid oversimplification. Science for the lay-child does not engage our imaginations just because it does not tell us things hard enough, new enough, important enough, adult enough. More important, it does not discipline our imaginations, because it does not discover (by its manner, its order, its allusions) the significance of these things to an adult mind. No more does science for the lay-scientist. Science for the layman proper, popularization, could be a very rewarding kind of writing and knowledge; it must inevitably be very necessary; but because we have not created, in both writer and reader (in a corporate critical consciousness they all share), some sense of who and what a layman is, it has not yet, it may never, come into full being.

II

I was reading in the philosophy of science, meanwhile, for answers to the larger questions and objections to what I was doing. What I needed most of all was some assurance that science could be profitably approached from my point of view – with the imagination, that is. That it was one of the humanities. That it could have something to give me, a non-scientist, and could play a part in my general education, redressing the balance of a sensibility grown so lop-sided.

Among the philosophers of science, Stephen Toulmin and Michael Polanyi afford most sustenance and encouragement to people making that pilgrimage. The latter's Personal Knowledge, *which few people seem to have read, is a remarkably rich and eloquent argument.*

The heart of the book is a philosophical attack on the objectivist theory of scientific knowledge, which it holds ultimately responsible for the enfeeblement of Western liberalism. Science has been made (this fallacy, too, Polanyi attacks) *the ideal form of all knowledge in the West; and on it is based a crippling and absurd demand for perfect objectivity in every form of intellectual life, including religion and politics.*

Theories of classical physics, says Polanyi, can be verified or falsified by an appeal to empirical evidence, but very little else can, even in science. Empirical evidence alone has never constituted scientific proof; the beliefs in astrology and witchcraft had a great deal of evidence to support them; far more than there could be against them. The Copernican revolution satisfied people's reason, not their senses; indeed, it went against their senses. Einstein, too, had no new facts, no observations, to offer, but a new rational scheme; and when opponents, authoritative opponents, brought factual evidence against that (some was presented by D. C. Miller when he was President of the American Physical Society in 1925) it was dismissed by the scientific world as a whole. Evidence alone, outside a structure of belief, is of small value scientifically.

Moreover, even science, though much the most purely logical form of knowledge, has its own passions; lives by them. Both the heuristic and the controversial passions are essential components of science, and researchers do not work simply by doubting their own or other people's propositions. Doubt can, of course, be a heuristic principle, but so can faith; Max von Laue discovered the diffraction of X-rays by crystals because he believed more completely, more concretely, than other people in the theoretical picture of crystals and rays they all shared.

Nor can logical simplicity be made the essential criterion; de Broglie's thesis on the wave-theory of matter so puzzled its official readers that they sent it to Einstein for a judgement on whether it made sense. Such a theory can be said to be simple only as a result of, as a part of, its being said to be true. It is the simplest statement of a complex reality – once we accept that complexity as really there. We must accept a different and more metaphysical idea of truth. We can only explain the validity of even scientific theories by admitting the idea that they make contact with a hidden reality.

We have been told to think of science as just the most economical description of a set of facts, or as just a set of working hypotheses, or as just a policy for drawing empirical inferences; to accord with our objectivism. But we must learn to think of it as the discovery of a hidden reality. Simplicity, symmetry, economy, are the marks of rationality, not the marks of truth as a whole, even scientific truth. We cannot account for our *acceptance of scientific theories without acknowledging our response also to their beauty and their profundity, two other categories of reality, and not objectively knowable.*

Moreover, Polanyi says, all knowledge is an active *comprehension of the thing known, an action that requires skill. Skilful knowing is like skilful doing; both are performed by subordinating a set of particulars, either as clues or tools, to the shaping of a skilful achievement, whether theoretical or practical. We then become subsidiarily aware of these particulars, within our focal awareness of the coherent entity. We do not observe them in themselves. Thus acts of comprehension are (in some ways) irreversible and (in that sense) non-critical; they cannot be measured by purely objective standards; we cannot have a fixed framework within which to reshape and test every act of knowledge. The modern demand for objectivity is thus a delusion we must drive out from our philosophy, and in so doing we shall renew the vitality of our political and cultural liberalism.*

My own ideas were, however, much less philosophical and political; they grew in the context of, under the protection of, Polanyi's and Toulmin's arguments, but when I came to put them together, in the talk that follows, it was surprising how indirectly that influence expressed itself. My arguments still centred themselves round concepts like 'imagination' and 'culture', and defined 'literature' and 'science' in relation to them.

A year of science

AFTER nearly two years of accepting the argument that there are two cultures, and in the middle of a year of full-time re-education along the lines that suggests, I re-read the 1959 Rede Lecture. I found it as convincing as ever as a general proposition, about society as a whole; and in its more personal application, to me as a teacher of literature (and, of course, to other such teachers), it was not *un*true. But I found that the terms in which I would put it have shifted somewhat over the two years.

I put it to myself these days that mine had been too purely literary an education, that a purely literary mind suffers from a dangerous imbalance; and that some scientific training could rescue me from that imbalance. A literary mind does not mean just someone with a degree in English. There is such a thing, surely, as *the* literary mind, a mode of the intelligence, in which we all participate from time to time if we have a grain of imagination; a mode of intelligence, with its characteristic subject-matter and set of interests, its characteristic logic and system, its characteristic set of values and indifferences and impatiences. The best examples are the great writers, and since the novel is the dominant form today, let us restrict ourselves to some great modern novelists; Proust, Kafka, Dostoevsky, Mann, Lawrence. Listed end to end they may seem rather various, but if we also make a list of great historians, or great physicists – Einstein, Rutherford, Bohr – that brings out an essential similarity between all performances of the literary mind. Its subject-matter is so much wider, for one thing. It ranges over far more of our experience. And all that experience is general; not average, of course, for Proust, Kafka, Dostoevsky do not deal with average experience. What, then, makes their subject-matter seem more general, less specialized, than the historians' or the physicists'? The fact surely that all this experience is personal, involving the individual as person, as unique, mysterious, an ultimate entity; not as a specimen, exemplifying one or other set of impersonal laws. This category is more general because it undercuts, underlies, a whole series of other, mutually exclusive, categories, like history, physics, psychology. And the logic by which the writer moves from point to point of this material is personal in the same sense; and the values he accords to what he finds are personal.

This intelligence has in our time created some major works of art, which must be discussed within properly and limitedly critical categories. But it has also expressed itself, and in no minor way, in books like Dostoevsky's *Notes from the Underworld*, and Lawrence's *Fantasia of the Unconscious*, in Nietzsche's philosophy, and in some great criticism. What manifests itself within the work of art in skills of imitation, invention, formal patterning, etc., manifests itself in the other books in other skills – of definition, of generalization, of argument. But that mind is so much the same in all its manifestations that it makes some of the largest traditional distinctions, between the aesthetic and the philosophical, seem trivial

If not unreal. It is the same observation and penetration we find in all those books, fiction and non-fiction, the same insights into our personal and political relationships, the same dismissals as insignificant or dangerous of so much that society or science offers us with pride; the same dramatic, prophetic morality. It is all one mode of the intelligence, theoretically unsystematized, but organically very unified.

The critic and teacher of literature, too, must therefore operate in this mode – not in the act of criticism and teaching, generally, but always in what lies behind those, what licenses him to teach or to criticize. Every good reader participates in it – that is how he understands and responds to what he is reading. And a purely literary mind is one which operates exclusively in that mode. A literary person tends, that is, when he sees an old friend, meets a new family, boards a ship, sits in an air-raid shelter, goes to a political meeting, to see in those things what Lawrence, Kafka, Mann, Dostoevsky saw. Tends to; few have enough energy for that very often; but those are the moments towards which he lives, and the rest can seem diurnality and philistinism.

It requires no demonstration that this mode of intelligence is only one of several; and it challenges no question that its exponents have traditionally distrusted the other modes, and above all the scientific. That conflict has been familiar to us at least since the Renaissance, when Petrarch said, just like a modern teacher of literature, that it was not Nature but human nature you should be studying, if you cared to know how to live. But there are differences between the character of conflict in Petrarch's time and its character today, some of which make it more serious. The first is the alarming success of modern science; the second is the alarming stature of modern literature. The word alarming means something different in that second use, but I offer it seriously. Both modes of intelligence have developed enormously and dangerously in their two opposite directions. The last fifty or hundred years, it seems to me, have produced a literature greater than any before; and more specifically literary. It has more to say about what constitutes the happiness and holiness of a person; and what it says is much more explosive.

One consequence of this parallel-but-divergent development is the inaccessibility of modern literature to scientists and vice versa. This is the phenomenon which Snow called the two cultures; and which might also be called the two half-cultures, since its worst feature is that neither side – no one at all – has a clear idea of the whole man, the man who knows enough of both to count himself a full citizen. One proof of that lies in the popularized science books, whose writers clearly have no idea of who their reader is to be, except that he won't be of the first intelligence. This is the fault of the literary men mostly, for they legislate the realm of discourse. Voltaire *created* the broadly-educated eighteenth-century intelligent layman, in the act of explaining Newton to his readers; and in the nineteenth century George Eliot achieved a breadth of tone we regard as now impossible, through a breadth of reference which authorized her to speak for the whole educated mind of her day. And the main scientific ideas of today are no more difficult to grasp than Newton's were in his time. There is a similar world-picture today, a scheme of large general ideas, which we all potentially share, and which could be the source of a similar largeness of mind and sureness of tone for us. But there is no general attempt today, among educated people, to share that picture, and it is Snow's attempt at that tone today which has most discredited him among the intelligentsia. To overcome that prejudice in myself, to apprehend the world-picture, is the more general, the more external benefit I might derive from this year, of science. To explain the other one, we must go back to the specialized quality of modern literature, and therefore of literary training today.

Lionel Trilling recently described the uniquely difficult, demanding, challenging, corrosive quality of modern literature. Corrosive because it makes the reader feel that anything less than spiritual heroism, spiritual extravagance, is inadequate. Professor Trilling says that the chief impulse of all modern literature is 'to surrender oneself to experience without regard to self-interest or conventional morality' – and that the effect of that is really to free oneself from social participation altogether. No other literature, he says, was ever so shockingly personal and spiritual, so uniquely concerned with the salvation of the individual. It is in this sense that it is more literary than other literatures. Trilling also points out that for many students no ideas that they will encounter in any college discipline will equal in force and sanction the ideas conveyed to them by modern literature; because of 'the agreement, ever growing in assertiveness, that art yields more truth than any other intellectual activity'. It is in this sense – among others – that it is greater than other literatures.

Because of this greatness, and perhaps also because other sources of authority have declined – the social, the political, the religious – the literary mind has unique power today. People believe James Joyce's account of Dublin in 1904 rather than that of a Lord-Lieutenant of Ireland at the time or an Archbishop of Dublin. And any representative of the literary mind – teacher or critic or good reader – enjoys a proportionate power. He has insights into the people and world around him that command the deference and discomfort of his acquaintance. Any university teacher of English can be the mediator of more of the revolutionary truths of adulthood to his students than the teacher of any other subject. In his comments on their essays, for instance, he can bring to bear on their own minds and experience the burning scrutiny of that great literature – by his references, by his examples, by his very vocabulary. And we find examples of this mode of intelligence raised to the power of heroism – its own kind of heroism – in achievements and whole careers prominent in the general world. It is *the* characteristic modern mode of heroism of the mind. The greatest of modern critics, Dr Leavis, and of modern political essayists, George Orwell, are the great examples for me.

With such intensity generated, such power endowed, it is clear that if there is any imbalance it will be dangerous. But, the obvious objection, is not such imbalance a matter of individual temperament? How can it be the result of that training itself? The literary mind as just defined is almost infinitely broad in its interests. The man with literary training finds that it applies itself to every new situation he gets into; and it is a passport into the other arts, into history, into a good half of psychology.

It is true that the literary mind has enormous scope as well as intensity. Its special narrowness is a function of those two together. It is exactly because literary intuitions carry us so far so fast nowadays that the things they cannot grasp lose all status for us, all dignity, all interest. What are those things? The best example I know occurs in D. H. Lawrence's *Kangaroo*. Lawrence relied on the literary mind more exclusively than any other writer, and it served him perhaps more magnificently. The houses, the towns, the bush, the people, everything he describes and everything he declares about Australia convinces us; until he comes to the political party, its aims, its origins, its strengths and weaknesses, its success and failure. And there, I think, we do not believe a word of it. Not because of its unlikelihood in a newspaper-factual sense; not what we might feel about *The Plumed Serpent*, for instance; Lawrence gives us details of the organization which seem reasonable enough, at least to me. It is simply, but completely, that his intuition has no authority on this subject. On quite internal evidence, by the movement of the prose, for instance, we know that he is inventing. He has taken political events out of their context, and reinterpreted them so radically they cease to *be* political events; not only in what he imagines for this novel, but in the general mass of his 'political' experience which is here given shape by his imagination.

For the modern literary mind is so personal, so obsessed with the salvation of individuals, that it has no respect – or insufficient respect – for any facts that are not relevant to that issue. For instance, for political and organizational problems of the kind *Kangaroo* tries to handle; consciously, intentionally, Lawrence was most respectful of his theme, but at a deeper level, where he had committed himself to the literary mode of intellection, he could not feel it as directly and vitally as he felt everything else. He translated it into other terms and dealt with it metaphorically. That is why, for instance, there are so few accidents, so few impersonal events, in his novels. What is not morally meaningful, not an act in a person's search for salvation, is so uninteresting it ceases to exist. Or rather, such things should cease to exist. In reality, brute facts continue to obtrude, after they have been dismissed from the literary mind; political and economic facts continue to control much of life, and this is the source of a hysteria about public affairs characteristic of that mind.

That hysteria of tone and poverty of experience is what I had begun to detect in my own mind. A fact that affected ten thousand people seemed less important to me, because less vivid, than the same fact affecting just one. I was bored, involuntarily, with political and economic problems. I was impatient that they should be settled, I realized, so that I could concentrate on what was really serious, really interesting – personal truths.

At the same time, examples of real breadth of mind in other people were coming to seem more and more attractive. One comes up against this problem in reading, for instance, the Holmes-Laski correspondence. These letters are a monument to two energetic, effective, honourable, useful, happy lives; fully responsible for, as well as responsive to, the world around them, and with no trace of the literary mind's fever. What a contrast with, say, Lawrence's letters.

If you have to choose between them, I would still choose Lawrence. Holmes and Laski could not read great modern literature. They preferred the easier, duller, feebler writers of their time; and thereby they cheated themselves of the fullest impact of their own personal experience. But, as you keep asking as you read the book, why can't you have both kinds of intelligence, and a full range of experience?

That there is such a problem, many people would agree. Far more than agree with my solution. A year of science seems to them, reasonably enough, like a bizarre and arbitrary choice among the paths that might lead to that destination. For my attempt to have the advantages of Holmes' and Laski's kind of intelligence, I have equipped myself with textbooks full of formulae and notebooks ready to have those formulae copied into them. How is that going to help me towards breadth of mind? Why bio-chemistry? Why not history, or political theory, or sociology? Well, it is not bio-chemistry instead of history, but as well as. That, however, still leaves a primacy to be explained. Why should chemistry or physics be studied full-time, while the other subjects are left to part-time reading? Why should they be there at all?

My answers to those questions I myself find puzzling. Not that I have no arguments to support them, or weak ones; the trouble is rather that I have too many, too large, too sweeping. They sweep away people I can't afford to have dismissed, they explain away as wrong things that are obviously right, important, beautiful – things in the world of modern literature, for example. Eliot's attitude to modern society, Lawrence's to modern science, are not simply wrong. What is needed is to introduce a new and important factor into our present response to them. My ideas will be valid only when they work with, interact completely with, the other factors in that response.

Everyone who reads literature nowadays with excitement has to face this problem; and must find, must have found, their own, different, ways to broaden and steady that set of responses aroused and trained there. Some seem to achieve it by political work, some by an intelligent worldliness and careerism, some by a deeper scholarship, most perhaps by a concern for education and culture. My solution, being more radical, must provoke opposition, and must have larger reasons, even though that largeness is so dangerous. The problem is complicated.

It is after all those with an acutely and primarily literary sensibility who will suffer most from this imbalance. If one's mind is as open to other modes of intelligence – the scientific or the historical – then this analysis need not apply. If you are as much a scientist or an historian as a man of literature, then this imbalance of sensibility has every chance of compensating for itself in your own mind. But the really intense and pure imagination, this is the difficulty, has a way of transcending its own limitations. One must not expect to find first-class men, in whatever line, neatly exemplifying a theory; much more a theory of their own limitedness. Eliot and Lawrence have ways of being non-'literary' – with a power, with a thoroughness, with a brilliance – that transcend any theory of what that word means, much more mine. The problem is complicated. But not insoluble. Eliot and Lawrence also have ways of being literary that do answer to this theory, and those ways are what we are discussing, because they are what we, all of us who are literary, share.

These apologies and self-encouragements over, I will offer three reasons why some scientific training could be a major route to that destination I'll assume we all aim at, a full free intelligence. First of all, because science is *the* other great intellectual discipline today; the only one that is comparable in power, that can arrest a self-confident mind in its too-intuitive judgements, moderate its too-impulsive movements. If the literary mind has a gift of fire today, so has the scientific mind. Science is the power and magic of today; literature is the sense of inspiration and prophecy. An imaginative man needs both, needs to participate in contemporary science in the sense in which a reader participates in contemporary literature.

Moreover, the scientific mind is embodied in enormous laboratories, dams, power plants, industries, enormous government grants, enormous numbers of people employed. All this is the embodiment and achievement of the intellect, in a sense that does not apply to commerce or administration; the intellect as distinct from the soul or common sense, much more the belly and the members. Compared with this, how meagre and shabby are the social insignia of other kinds of intellectual work – of literature, for instance. Anyone who calls himself an intellectual needs to feel some likeness between his own work and work that is so largely, simply, generally, revered. Otherwise he will feel an exaggerated and debilitating sense of his own neglect.

Secondly, because science is a body of vital information as well as a discipline. We cannot respond in any vigorous and masculine way even to traditional things like the sea and sky unless we know them factually, according to contemporary categories, as contemporary facts, not as occasions for sensibility. Much less can we respond to the new, man-made things, the great machines, the texture and substance of modern life, unless we know enough about it to accept it emotionally as our own creation, not theirs, the others', the enemies'.

Even in lyrical literary description scientific information is necessary to a modern writer, or is a great help. Proust, Lawrence, Nabokov, these are the modern novelists whose evocation of Nature one remembers, whose response was most authoritative, and surely that is because they all employ some scientific precision, use some scientific categories, in their descriptions. The appeal to classical legends – as in, say, E. M. Forster – has been less successful. If our imaginations are to work on the stars, the sea, the flowers, in any vigorous way, we must know things about them; and some of the things to know are nowadays scientific facts. And for the artificial structures of civilization, this is even more true. Culture has been an entity in opposition to the new social facts and the new mechanical and scientific facts in their social applications, ever since the idea of culture was invented. That is why Snow was quite justified in assuming a close connection, an identification, between science and technology. For cultured people they *are* so identified – as The Others, the great hostile force that is running away with civilization.

Thirdly, above all, because at the heart of all science is the impersonal mode of experience, literature's natural and only complement. I don't mean so much that massive otherness, that incorruptible impersonality of the great physical or mathematical problems which both Einstein and Planck have talked about. I am thinking of the subtle penetration of even the most intimately personal experience by an impersonal mode of feeling. Even the experience of pain, for instance; something in my pain is uniquely, ungeneralizably mine, but something is common to all men, and that is interesting, too. Known in this mode, the individual is not unique and mysterious; he is an animal entity in a material cosmos, an organization of appetites and aptitudes identical with others of his species. And these facts are as vivid and exciting, as real and true, as important, about oneself, to oneself, as the personal facts.

The purely literary mind, as I said, cannot grasp the idea of ten thousand people. It can hardly count above two or three. Certainly if something personal is said to be true of twenty people – some precisely identified emotion or state of mind – you know this is somewhat rhetorical. Indeed, the facts of general, socially significant misery – hunger, disease, unemployment – are too abstract for a literary imagination even in relation to one person. The reader cannot focus his eye on them; they are too large, too blank; rhetorical. They have to stay on the fringe of the picture.

One has to focus on how they interact with more intricate, more properly personal conditions – how the hungry man's feelings about his friends change.

And in the world outside, too, anyone who has read modern literature as passionately as it asks and deserves to be read, will find his eye swerving away from facts he wants to focus on, slipping off the surface of truths he feels are crucial. This has happened so generally, over the last fifty years, that our culture now lacks any integrated body of intellectual experience that includes both the really powerful categories – the scientific and the literary. But even more immediately and personally disconcerting is to realize that the literary sensibility, which is the site of most acute moral sensation for most educated people these days, used in their daily lives, is by itself a somewhat distorting instrument, and in some sense an impoverisher of experience.

Some elementary scientific training has seemed to me the way to rescue my own fragment of that mind. Obviously, it remains something of a gamble.

I considered other ways of arguing my point, besides those I finally included in that talk. There is, for instance, a sense in which the two cultures today assume secondary sexual characters in some people, to some extent polarize all men's intellectual natures into masculine and feminine. When I hear Robert Lowell say his country (meaning its political leaders) may destroy the world because of a fatal simplicity in their minds, I think how many women find men fatally simple; and isn't that because men have to take and execute decisions, of which women have to watch the untidy and un-satisfying consequences? And isn't that complexity the poet prizes the result of his feminine role? Poets and novelists, but also critics and teachers of literature, are all in some sense forced into a feminine role by contrast with scientists. Theirs are the domestic arts; like embroidery. In time of war, of any national emergency, men are expected to lay aside their culture, and even their intellectual honesty in the Orwellian sense. In war literary men can best serve their country as cannon fodder; but the scientist is spurred on to greater efforts in his laboratory, to more research and more experiment. Even in peace-time, as Father Gerald Vann says in The Paradise Tree, *our civilization stresses the masculine (which he identifies quite explicitly*

*with the scientific and technological) at the expense of the feminine-reflective
(the literary and aesthetic). It is my argument, of course, that the literary
man's reaction to such home-truths has been too much to become more
'feminine-reflective', in one or other violent or vitriolic manner; it* should
have been to re-establish his temperamental balance by participating to some
extent in the masculine mode. But the point to be argued first is the justice
of this analysis of the sexual distribution. Presumably the pure scientist at
the moment of creative effort is no more to be called masculine or feminine
than the great novelist at his. Both are thinking very strenuously and
methodically, both are employing intuition as well as traditional method,
both must be aware of much past and contemporary work while also con-
sulting only themselves. But I was struck, when I took my physics and
maths courses, by the number of problems which involved calculations in
road-banking and bridge-building and explosives' power; which I contrasted with the exploration of say Salome's psychology or Millamant's
social position which might be being required of the literary student in the
next classroom. There is, in this sense, a sexual character to each as
branches of study; which is carried further by the contrasting characters of
professional demonstration in each, which in literature is so much more a
matter of appeal than in science, more dependent on the personal understanding and general sympathies of those involved; and as a creative social
force, it is, of course, science, not literature, which is allied with war and
industry and transformations of the environment. This sexual polarization
is a curious and sometimes poignant example of the antinomies and conflicts
generated by the cultural split, which can lead in particular cases to quite
personal suffering. (In most people, of course, this intellectual sexuality will
be compensated for without conscious strain, but where there was imbalance
before the problem may be felt.) The scientist can suffer from a sense of
personal aridity, the literary man from ineffectuality or hysteria.*

*Science does contain, moreover, the kind of truth I suspect most non-
scientists simply do not know is there. I mean truths that satisfy the
imagination as fully, as many-sidedly, as immediately (if one has some
scientific preparation) as literary truths. This occurs vividly where mathematical and physical or chemical facts come together. For instance, when
we realize that a major formula in pure mathematics also describes the
curve any chain forms itself into when it is allowed to hang freely (the
catenary curve, which is the locus of an important equation) or that a*

complicated piece of pure geometry also tells us about (actually helped discover) the arrangement of atoms in a crystal. But equally vivid cases occur within mathematics itself; the formula $e^{\pi i} = -1$, for instance. That so many of the great mathematical constants should multiply out to negative unity is surely exciting and satisfying in a purely imaginative way. It evokes the whole history of mathematics, from the Greeks on; it evokes the essential nature of mathematics, in which those symbols have been so variously employed; while both by its simplicity of style and by its statement it concentrates all those memories, and fuses them with the beauty of the largest kind of pattern.

Above all, however, ours is a scientific civilization, and we must be able to respond to so large a fact with something better than a wish it weren't so — better even though that wish have tragic intensity and scope. What distinguishes our age from earlier ones is clearly that we have more tremendous powers at our disposal, powers created by science. And this new endowment is clearly the natural necessary consequence of our being who we are. For what has distinguished our whole post-Hellenic culture from others, from the Chinese, the Indian, the Mayan, is our achievement in science. It was the creation of a mathematical astronomy (typified in the Almagest), the fusion of mathematics and physics, which marked the beginning of our culture, as Derek de Solla Price says in Science Since Babylon. *China had both the two kinds of mathematics that came together in the Hellenic cities, the geometric, logical, and pictorial mathematics of the ancient Greeks, and the arithmetical and quantitative kind of the Babylonians, but Chinese mathematics formed no link with the natural sciences. That link, that infinitely creative liaison and its effects in practical life, has characterized our culture more than anything else; that plus the high technological content of our science, which became important with the second great beginning in mathematical astronomy, the Copernican-Newtonian revolution. These together, which are what we mean by science, have characterized our society, and distinguished it from all other; even more than our Christianity. As time goes by, this becomes more and more true. That is above all why, at a crude level, we must learn some science; why, at a deeper level, we must each work out the relationship of his own work to scientific work; why, deeper still, we must work out what a culture is, of which 'science' can be such a huge branch.*

3. An exploratory essay

This next chapter sums up the experience of my year at Cambridge, and is the book's biggest single attempt at analysing the problem into my own terms; an analysis which does not differ from (at least, does not consciously disagree with) Snow's or Polanyi's – or Toulmin's or Williams's. They, of course, talk about quite different things, one from another, and disagree, sharply, in their estimates of some of those points they do all discuss. But from my point of view their main ideas all potentially converge; indeed, the point where they seem to meet is where I build this argument.

My essay talks of 'humanism' so much I must insist in advance this means nothing like the fruity-voiced gentlemanliness one associates with administrators addressing an academic audience. That, obviously, is the decadent relic of an earlier, Edwardian humanism, which even in a livelier form we could not revive today. Nor is it like the humanism of Irving Babbitt, which consisted of a

familiarity with that golden chain of masterpieces which links together into a single tradition the more permanent experience of the race; books which so agree in essentials that they seem, as Emerson puts it, to be the work of one all-seeing, all-hearing gentleman.

The books we must be familiar with do not seem the work of any one man, nor of any number of gentlemen; they do not link together into any golden chain; there is little that is reassuring or mellowing or helpful about them.[1]

The modern humanism we need cannot be fully specified here and now, because it could take any of several forms, but it will surely be something terser, more astringent, more strenuous than either of those, something which has faced the challenges of modern literature and modern science, has

---

[1] Babbitt's humanism took its rise in part from a hostility to science.

accepted their criteria of truth, of honesty, of discipline, of relevance – has
understood and accepted their account of life today.

Understandably, it is among scientists, and not among literary men
(providing we consider only the liveliest minds in the two disciplines), that
we find an older humanism still surviving. Thus Professor Oppenheimer
writes, in Science and the Common Understanding,

We must talk of our subject . . . as men concerned with understanding,
through analogy, description, and an act of confidence and trust, what other
men have done and thought and found. So men listen to accounts of soldiers
returning from a campaign of unparalleled hardship and heroism, or of ex-
plorers from the high Himalayas, or of tales of deep illness, or of a mystic's
communion with his God.

Here we recognize the old chart of human experience, of heroic types. The
explorer (from the high Himalayas), the mystic, the soldier, all in picturesque
costume and posture, engraved on embossed and creamy paper. And we hear
the same voice from Professor Needham in History is on Our Side.
After quoting from a seventeenth-century book, which he had been reading
out in the country near Cambridge, he muses,

An excellent conceit. Far away in the distance there was the implacable hum
of a tractor, harvesting on a farm towards Horningsea, speaking a language
symbolic of the future, a language of tremendous possibilities, but sometimes
seeming too alien from the past and the ideas of the past. How difficult to
translate into it the spiritual and intellectual beauties which the men of the
past found it worth while to live for. The task would try to the uttermost, I
thought, even the interpretative powers of Lancelot Andrews.

This is exactly the kind of writing, and attitude to experience, which I
was offered at school as culture itself, and which I learned at the university
to reject, to read as the sign of a flabby mind. Obviously it is not the sign of
any such thing in Professor Oppenheimer and Professor Needham, but
neither is that diagnosis in general invalid. Language (in the sense of
general educated style) changes and develops according to its own autono-
mous laws, and certain forms of speech, like these, which were once employed
by highly intelligent men, now bear a mark which warns off the wary today.
Scientists, not being professionally expert in the language of general dis-
course, sometimes mistake these marks, and use out-of-date forms which
betray their general meaning, belie their real intelligence. An arts man, or

at least a literary man, would know in the first sentence of such a passage that his language was falsifying his thought, that the humanistic attitudes he was assuming, the verbal gestures he was making, are the prescriptive mark now of the retired and pensioned-off mind. That is why the responsibility for healing the two cultures wound lies more with the literary man – because the language of general discourse is his concern. But what kind of humanistic attitude can he assume? Those old gestures we have all rejected without regret, that graceful turn of the phrase, that noble turn of the head, that polished quotation, but in favour of what? On the whole, I claim (there will always be exceptions, of course), in favour of anti-humanism, the pure, intense, unrelatable truths of modern literature and modern science.

Return to Cambridge

I have been taking undergraduate courses again this year, and by coincidence I was at the university where I was first an undergraduate, sixteen years ago. This gives me a chance to catch up with that part of my past which is vaguest in my memory. I remember the years before 1945 and after 1948 a good deal more clearly than those three themselves, and this vagueness of memory derives, I think, from a vagueness in the events of my undergraduate life. By the events I mean the lectures, supervisions, and every kind of official encounter, with tutor, porter, etc., but also the various clubs and magazines and sports, and the whole complex of semi-personal relations that make up the Cambridge part of one's life here. There was a vagueness in these events because neither I nor the other people were quite naturally engaged in them. Both I and the university (in its representatives) were playing parts which allowed us very little chance to say, or ask, the really relevant things.

For instance, I remember a supervision where one of my companions read out his paper on the progress of the Western mind since the Reformation, in the form of a fable about a breed of gastropod molluscs for ever climbing up the sides of a glass container and for ever slipping back. The author – a recent convert to Roman Catholicism – had impressive connections with a salon-keeping Sicilian countess, and the paper was both written and read in a formidably polished and professional manner. Even at the time, I think, I was ironical about this in conversation, but at a deeper level I was dismayed. Another time, when we were reading the Romantics, we were recommended to attempt lyrics in imitation of Keats, Shelley, Byron; this time it was I who read out my week's work, and this time I felt almost consciously betrayed and angry. In both cases the events were ultimately unreal to me; both in the theatricality of the gestures I found myself performing, and because of the unconscious dismay they aroused in me and which flavoured all my conscious feelings about it.

My point is that my supervisor was not the man to be simple-mindedly impressed by brilliant performances in that genre, and I, though blindly then, particularly distrust them. But the situation in which we found ourselves demanded brilliance − the alternative apparently was dullness. Knowing about the Romantics was something we already knew about; we owed it to ourselves to do better than that; we needed to perform in some way. We could not believe soberly in what we were doing at the university; our manner was overexcited because our feeling was false.

Something similar happened in several areas of my Cambridge life, and they added up to this strain of unreality and vagueness − the anger was quite latent − in my experience. I felt I was taking part in a masque of theatrical stylishness; called on to pretend I had a quite unreal (to me) personality and interests − intellectually, that I participated in a very rounded, serene, bright-coloured world-picture, like an old-fashioned heraldic map; while at the same time all the voices of real authority spoke to me of something quite opposite. So that one constantly found oneself, as in those supervisions, acting a part one did not believe in, deep down, and consequently missing one's cues. What makes this interesting to me now is that I think that if I were eighteen again the same thing could happen, despite the changes here since 1948; and that although some of the artificiality was Cambridge's, the problem would be somewhat the same at other English universities. It is one symptom of a disease of our times.

That disease can be called the decay or the corruption of humanism. To be a generally well-educated person is not a satisfying aim for a student alive to the messages in the air today. It does not mean knowing the things that are worth knowing, or exercising the powers one wants to exercise. One has to go further, to be clever or serious in some other way − at the expense, ultimately, of *that* aim, and therefore of the idea of a university itself. For a university, at least in the West, has to create the idea of an educated person as something complete and splendid in itself, something that can by itself evoke both a lively and a steady enthusiasm. And therefore it has to be a manifestation of humanism; meaning a community of interests and investigations, into different subjects, but all (in so far as they are humanistic) identical in the way they involve the intelligence; engaging a man's intellect at its most intensely efficient and therefore its most ruthlessly specialized, but also, and equally, as the servant of the total human mind, with all that includes of non-intellectual and indeed contra-rational powers. Humanism's most characteristic movement and mood is to visit different branches of knowledge authoritatively, to discover likenesses and relationships between them, and to expand in the excitement of so much successful human activity. It is not, however, to compare the present patronizingly with the past, or to mint noble platitudes, or to expand in the consciousness of names and dates known as if they were turkey and pudding swelling one's intellectual stomach. That is our modern puritan caricature of humanism. It is part of our licence to remain specialists or adventurers of the intellectual life; scholarly specialists or anti-scholarly adventurers – grinding a political, a religious, or just a careerist axe. (It was under the inspiration of some such late, decadent, and gaudy humanism, consciously old-fashioned, that our supervision attempted its clumsy gestures at brilliance, which were doomed so inevitably to discredit that inspiration and that ideal.) But unless humanism can mean something more than that now, and that something can be realized in university life, lively students must find the elaborate structure of colleges and clubs offensive, and must aim at some more serious (or eccentric) outreaching of it. This must be particularly true at Oxford and Cambridge, where that structure is more elaborate then elsewhere.

The most striking examples of this decay in academic work itself occur in literary and scientific studies. In both of these, elements have emerged during the last hundred years which deserve to be called – though for very different reasons – antihumanist. These elements are at least as brilliant and serious as any others in their subject-areas, and they are the characteristically modern ones. I have more to say about them later, but for the moment I want to call attention only to the overwhelming success of these particular studies in modern times, and to their inordinate influence on other disciplines. Anyone who is not underprivileged mentally must count his first successful reading of Lawrence or Kafka or Proust or Dostoevsky one of his great experiences. And anyone who does not close his eyes and ears intellectually must feel the year-by-year achievements of modern physics as a continuing excitement as well as threat. The arts in general have accompanied literature into the eccentric, the obscure, the esoteric; and the social sciences have imitated science in their methods and language. And in those broader disciplines which stand midway between the extreme personalness of modern literature and the extreme impersonalness of modern science, in history, philosophy, the humanities proper, it is often easy to trace the influence of one or other of those magnetic poles. In philosophy, for instance, it is easy to trace the literary influence on the Existentialists, and the scientific influence on the Positivists.[1] And in *What is History?* E. H. Carr makes the same distinctions in that subject; he draws up lists of literary writers of history – those interested primarily in personalities – and reserves his praise for those scientific historians who deal with impersonal forces. For him the word literature seems to mean story books.

Mr Carr's, and Dr Needham's, vigorous history-making may seem to constitute a very important objection to a phrase like 'the decay of humanism'. But their vigour, though it makes their subject almost the liveliest of the humanities, has a non-humanist, indeed an anti-humanist, cast. I am not saying that Marxism is inevitably anti-humanist, but that it has been and is anti-literary, anti-aesthetic, and quite powerfully so. Both writers' references to literature (Dr Needham says that of course poets hate analysis, for instance) show a very thin theory of what literature now is. No philosophy, however vigorous, which denies or ignores one of

---

[1] It is interesting also to speculate on the share of Wittgenstein's intellectual glamour which he owed to his characteristically modern and anti-humanist personality.

the two major modes of contemporary thought, can be called a humanism.

The other general, philosophical movement of modern times, which has attempted to unite great areas of knowledge, may be called neo-Catholicism. If we take T. S. Eliot as a representative of this, we must admit that it has a profound understanding of modern literature. It needs no proof, however, that he and the other Christian humanists have had no helpful understanding of, no exciting response to, modern science and the changes in modern life that that is bringing.

To find the voice of a true humanism we have to go back to before the First World War, to writers like Whitehead, Forster, and Santayana, who both were first-rank professionals in their own lines, and also accepted the responsibility to rationalize all human experience; of course, other people since then have accepted that challenge, but what distinguishes those three is the serenity and breadth and openness of tone with which they discussed and discharged their responsibility. A serenity which looks to us like over-innocence, or even, at first glance, simple optimism, but which is, in fact, humanism in action; a confident, confiding appeal to a community of interests and values in the educated world at large.

We must, of course, admit that there was something unreal in their confidence, a slightly out-of-date quality in their minds. This can be located conveniently in their descriptions of England, of its universities, of Cambridge; for all their marvellous liberality and energy of sympathy, the England they describe is exclusively southern and pastoral, over-ripe, over-historical, over-beautiful; and in their descriptions of university life there is so little experience of personal anger or irony. This is not complacency in them, much less stupidity; it is simply innocence. A slightly guilty innocence, however, because authoritative voices had already been raised, in which the more savage ironies and tensions of modern experience had been asserted. Their innocence was not corrupt, but it was slightly hollow and static and fragile. Theirs was a true humanism, but it was at the point where a change was needed, in spirit as well as form. A contemporary version would have to be radically different.

Exactly this humanism persisted after 1914, however, not only in the forms of university life, but also in the spirit of ordinary academic work, even of some of the best work in subjects like history and political theory; but it became more and more old-fashioned. Its scope was gradually narrowed, its energy insensibly sapped. No humanistic response to the facts of Marxism and Nazism, and the behaviour of the two régimes, seemed adequate. Humanism at its most vigorous must be a matter mostly of knowing, of understanding, and in its decay it does not rise above mere appreciation and personal stylishness. People in the Thirties felt they had to act, even intellectually, to commit themselves; their ideas had to be extreme. You can trace this development in the Holmes-Laski letters; Holmes, in his old age, coming to represent the extreme decay of humanism into a disbelief in any kind of intellectual action; Laski, in his response to the times, moving further and further to the left, towards a more drastic philosophy. Neither could any longer invest energy, concentrated effort, hard work, in their humanism. And you can also trace the hidden causes of this development; the failure of that old-fashioned version to take any successful account of either modern literature or modern science, both of which were more in accord with the events of the day than the humanities proper were. This failure reduced the humanism of Laski and Holmes too much to gossips about first-editions and re-readings of the classics. This was bound to alienate someone of the next generation, as frivolous, self-indulgent, and pompous.

I began as an undergraduate in 1945, when the atomic bombs had just been dropped on Hiroshima and Nagasaki, and Belsen and Buchenwald had just been liberated and photographed. In other ways, too, my experience, though inarticulate, was of my century. The characters I met in Dickens and Thackeray led emotional lives very unlike mine. When, later, I read Lawrence and Kafka, I seemed to discover my own experience; I met those elements in my feelings which I hadn't heard about from other people; which I therefore hadn't till then named in myself, but whose unnamedness existed in my mind, blocking any full identification with what I did read.

At school, and in the extra-curricular reading suggested to us, the general scheme of things had been a faded version of that pre-1914 humanism. We read essays by Lamb and Hazlitt, Chesterton and Belloc, and composed elegant little exercises of the same kind ourselves. We studied Shakespeare, and let our fancies roam for three pages over the nature of Cleopatra's feeling for Antony. As outside reading in history we were recommended Philip Guedalla and Carola Oman and Sacheverell Sitwell. In the school library we were given Hugh Walpole and Trollope. We knew there was such a thing as modern poetry, but it didn't seem to be what people read. Science I thought of as an endless continuation of School Cert. physics and chemistry, with some scientist who was also an inventor in his spare time (like an English master writing stories for Punch*) producing the bomb.*

For human excellence, we were told about Lawrence of Arabia and Scott of the Antarctic. We knew that Churchill was a great man and a great stylist; though he was also a wily politician. As war heroes I remember hearing more about Rupert Brooke and Wilfred Owen than about Second War soldiers.

I believed what I was told, but it was not fully meaningful to me; because this wasn't my kind of style, or my kind of courage, or my kind of greatness; because the elements in my experience which were to seem its essence – the twentieth-century elements – were not found in Lamb or Trollope or Churchill or Rupert Brooke. It is interesting that Laski was very excited by the story of Captain Scott, and classed it immediately with Drake's journey in the Golden Hind. *It illustrates how even the liveliest humanistic mind, since it was out of touch with modern literature, was also out of touch quite generally with its juniors, and enthusiastically endorsed legends like this, which could have no meaning for them. My own unresponsiveness was half consciously a resentment against something prepared for boys, or for 'the nation' – for other people. As, of course, the Lawrence of Arabia legend obviously was, and the Rupert Brooke legend – the last seems to have been launched largely in pieces by Churchill and Henry James, under the guidance of Edward Marsh. All these rang false, even before anything else had rung true.*

This was a humanism Cambridge allowed me to outreach ironically. In fact, it commanded me to. There was a great deal of such irony in the Cambridge air. Dons were returning from various kinds of war work. Some of them had seen Belsen and Buchenwald. The lively ones had undergone at some time or other a conversion away from humanism to Catholicism, or Communism, or Existentialism.

But at the same time the institutions of the place, Union debates and rowing clubs and college sermons and May balls, continued to proclaim a powerfully organized humanistic-ruling-class idea of Cambridge; as a place where no idea was too big to be placed in, and controlled by, a polite social context; and in our supervisions we practised those stylish gestures which outshone the ideas they expressed, which put every subject into an elegant perspective.

All this was for me, and must be for contemporary undergraduates, profoundly puzzling. My irony was a quite helpless reaction to the incompatibility of things. But it was taken as a determination to be clever. This was not, of course, disapproved of. It was expected, especially from someone in English. I was invited to perform, in a variety of ways, one of which was those supervision exercises. I was invited to join in the irony of others. But what I really wanted was to believe in something unironically, or in a way that could control, discipline, give meaning to, my irony. That I didn't get.

There is one exception to this, of course. I attended Dr Leavis's lectures and read what he wrote and read what he recommended. In him I found what I needed. But this did not help me to a beginning of humanism, or modify my latent alienation from the 'humanism' of Cambridge. It rather intensified that alienation.

Two or three years ago, when I was trying to explain how much I owed to those lectures, I hit on the phrase 'He taught me what to do with my intenser feelings', and that still sums up a great deal. Cambridge, the other dons, humanism, the conditions of educated intercourse, had seemed to afford no scope to those insights and irritabilities in which I recognized myself most.

Those insights and irritabilities were of a kind which I gradually found were the subject-matter of modern literature. For after the great achievements of Tolstoy and George Eliot, it seems, the realist tradition in the novel could no longer synthesize the elements of both external social-natural description and internal psychological-moral exploration. On the whole, the great writers since then have developed the second vein at the expense of the first. Writers like Kafka, Proust, Dostoevsky, Lawrence, describe the social scene in ways that ring true only to highly personal and unconventional feelings, that contradict all socially agreed or socially feasible interpretations. The truths they deal in are personal; often specifically anti-social. In Proust, for instance, the analysis of love and of personality reduces these entities to something quite unusable socially; if *that* is what love is, it has nothing to do with getting married, or even getting divorced. It has been writing of this sort, since 1870, which has produced the great things.

This period of literature has been perhaps greater than any in the past, and it has certainly been more ambitious. Writers have been the great truth-tellers, and have assumed moral and spiritual functions that were in the past the monopoly of philosophers and priests. At the same time its true scope is no wider, indeed narrower than before. The writer has relied more exclusively, and drawn more powerfully, on purely literary insights, and these have proved to be, though limitless in their energy, limited in their provenance to the world of personal feelings; meaning by personal that which relates to the nucleus of moral responsibility at the core of an individual. This can then include references to political and economic convictions, but literature will be interested only in that most religious strand in them for which a man can be totally praised or loved, that element which represents a free choice and which is an act of self-creation. It is interested in a man's membership of a political party in so far as that represents courage in *him*, or self-punishment – not for the purely political reasons.

Literature has also been purer in this century; purged of non-literary purposes. Joyce asked that his reader should devote his life to reading his novel. Nietzsche declared that art not ethics was man's essential metaphysical activity. No concessions were made to entertainment of social use or comprehensibility. Writers became the priests of an austere, difficult, demanding religion. It is no longer fashionable for writers to talk like this now, but those great achievements are there behind and around them. They ignore those ambitions only at the price of aiming low. We still live in the age of Lawrence and Kafka. The imagination of our literature changed with them, and it has not changed since.

This literature evoked a corresponding sensibility in its readers which has been anti-humanist in effect, not only because the old humanism had become so relaxed, timid, and philistine, and the new mood had to oppose it; but also because this new mood was so sharply personal, while any humanism depends on some kind of general, non-personal organization. Humanism is essentially a matter of organized investigation and comparison, of co-operation between scholars and critics, of teaching at an institution, of a ramified framework. But really to teach, say, Lawrence or Dostoevsky at a university is very difficult, because the books often demand whole-hearted sympathy for an anti-university point of view, and if you really engage in forcing your students to face the challenge of the novel, you raise the question of your own answer to that challenge. So you diminish either the writer or yourself or the teaching. The modern writer doesn't want to be taught or discussed. He is presenting insights that attack the central poise of the humanistic mind. Even a book like *The Catcher in the Rye*, so wonderfully effective in arousing the American student's sensibility, ends by making the teacher's role almost untenable. Lionel Trilling says that he used to solve these problems by dwelling on the formal properties of modern literature, its techniques and strategies, but that now he realizes that this is an evasion of the essential personal challenge of the material. All this would, of course, be clearer in America than in England, where universities do not teach so much modern or non-English literature. But the problem is only masked here. Our sensibilities have been changed, once for all, and even in a course in Shakespeare (or the Romantics of my supervision) sooner or later both students and teacher are going to feel that this is mere academicism if there is no scope for those pure intensities of feeling characteristic of the modern literary mind.

Of course, it is possible to generate those intensities while talking about Shakespeare. Dr Leavis does. He shows us how the study and criticism of literature can evoke the same excitement as the primary reading and writing of it. He does so by making his reading militant, by using it to attack other critics or other poets or something ugly in modern civilization; by his anti-academic and anti-contemporary posture. But even he masks the problem for us somewhat. He talks at length only about Lawrence, among modern writers, and in Lawrence he emphasizes the things he has in common with George Eliot, not the things he shares with Dostoevsky. This can be misleading. England is lucky in having probably the greatest of modern writers and the greatest of modern critics, and doubly lucky in that both of them maintain a lively connection with the great nineteenth-century past and a sense of responsibility for the country's culture as a whole. It is through them, if through anyone, that we shall find a way to include the destructive insights and moods of modern literature into a larger humanism. But we have to understand first that they are themselves typical modern figures, and typical in their anti-humanism. We have to reject in part their claim to be simply the inheritors of the nineteenth century. It is their anti-humanism, their intense hostility to the mass of their colleagues, their translation of cultural history into their own personal struggles, that makes them the heroes of our time, and gives Dr Leavis such a power over the imaginations even of those who disagree with him most seriously. He alone has known how to teach literature with the intensity with which it is now written. But it is no accident that he has taught it in opposition – personal, bitter, fanatical opposition – to all established order.

Physics has the same role in modern science as the novel has in modern literature. The scientific names to places besides Proust, Kafka, Dostoevsky, are Einstein, Rutherford, Heisenberg, Schrodinger, etc.; wave-mechanics, quantum-mechanics, relativity, atomic theory, etc. This is not to say that astronomy, chemistry, biology, have been unimportant in our time; but that (up to ten years ago) the most brilliant things have been achieved in physics, and have constituted the modern idea of science for all but specialists in other branches. The same could be said of poetry and the drama as compared with the novel; they have been dwarfed and subordinated, partly only in public estimation, but partly in reality. The main features of the idea thus constituted have been the disappearance of substance, the dominance of mathematics, the incomprehensibility of science to non-scientists, and the release of terrible powers.

Modern physics has presented itself as the ultimate achievement of the impersonal mode of knowledge, and thus as at the opposite extreme from modern literature. It was in the study of matter in motion that the objective, mathematicized, experimental method in science secured its first triumphs, and physics has been the scene of its most logical and irrefutable successes since; through three centuries during which the Western mind has come more and more under its influence. This social predominance of the impersonal mode of knowledge was at the source of literature's revulsion towards the extremely personal. The connection is made clear in Dostoevsky's seminal *Letters from the Underworld*; it is in protest against the claims of science, progress, logic, social planning, etc., that Dostoevsky proclaims the autonomy of man's irrational, non-moral, fundamentally spiritual, and above all *free* nature. In England the conjunction of the Industrial and Scientific Revolutions called forth a tradition of cultural criticism which – though perhaps this country's greatest intellectual achievement – was cripplingly on the defensive, setting literary, cultural, personal values in radical opposition to science and to modern life in general. But though this literature and this science are at opposite extremes from each other, they are both equally inaccessible to the average educated man, both equally recalcitrant to humanistic treatment.

Modern physics is just as pure as modern literature. Its consequences are terribly social but its purposes not at all, and the physicist works in an enclave insulated from the general world by its enormous machines, its highly trained population, its social position, above all its abstract language and thought. This insulation is a good deal more notable than it was in the last century, and a great deal more notable than it is now in subjects like history.

The terrible destructive powers released by modern science threaten humanism, in that they make us despair of finding any way to understand and talk about such things keenly enough and broadly enough to allay our fear and revulsion and renunciation of all understanding. But the anti-humanism of science is more strictly the difficulty of its language and methods, and the acceptance by scientists of their intellectual isolation. Those with a social conscience do attempt to explain their work, but usually to the man in the street. Humanism would be created only in a successful communication with their colleagues in other disciplines.

Of course, there are people like Schrodinger, whose *What is Life?* is a beautiful humanistic document. But it seems as if much more typical figures of modern science – at least in England – have been J. J. Thomson and Rutherford. These seem to be the names to put beside Lawrence and Leavis as the supreme exponents of the other great mode of modern intelligence, and they illustrate the other – very different – kind of anti-humanism. From what one can gather, the Cavendish tradition was in part anti-intellectual. One did one's work at the laboratory and went off to football and a detective novel.

The ideas of modern physics and the modern novel have a beauty, a purity, and a danger that can absorb the whole imagination of those who work on them. They are difficult to grasp in themselves, and difficult to bring into relation with any other kind of experience. Juxtaposed with our lax decadent humanism they have proved as destructive as radium. The imagination of our whole generation has been conditioned to respond only to pure, difficult, and dangerous truths.

During my three years at Cambridge I was therefore seeking (though at first unconsciously) just such extreme, partisan, and murderous truths. I went to Dr Leavis's lectures, I joined the Communist Society, I attended mass at Fisher House, I heard Evelyn Waugh speak on 'Back to the Catacombs'. The other side of Cambridge, the papers to write, the Tripos, a dinner with an editor, a sherry party with a MP, seemed necessary but ignoble machinery, to be got through with the minimum of personal involvement. There was no truth in such things, nothing but compromise, careerism, externality; official half-truths and popular myths. This is, of course, a common adolescent attitude to the grown-up world, and perhaps I would have felt it in any place or time. But there was, I claim, no voice with authority to instruct me in any alternative attitude.

Moreover, all this machinery (humanistic-ruling-class in its masterful mixing of different kinds of value) was treated quite similarly by the rest of Cambridge. Even those dons and undergraduates with no commitments to anti-social truths referred to exam results, Union elections, contacts with the great, with the same scepticism as I did. Or rather it seemed the same to me. In fact, perhaps theirs was the scepticism of the administrator, not the rebel. They, too, could not believe in the 'humanism' Cambridge so half-heartedly offered. But they could believe in the beauty and value and use of power. Oxford and Cambridge are full of that awareness of power to come; they are probably different in that way from universities in America, and certainly from the others in England. This makes it doubly important that humanism there should be massive, eloquent, full-voiced.

But when, in my third year, I went to the University Appointments Board to decide on what job I should apply for, I got an unpleasant shock; because I found there a university official who insisted on looking at the problem from the point of view of the employer, of the outside world. He took the official requirements of the BBC, the ICI, the Civil Service, etc., seriously, and expected that I do the same. He told me the story of the young man who told a bishop he thought he would take orders, and got the 'gentle' reply, 'Be sure that you get them, my son.' I was to think if I was good enough to get one of these jobs, and good enough not by some purely mechanical and external standard. All this was a real shock to me, and I imagine to many others, if they had had no family experience of the power-élite. I had never heard anyone take the public world on its own moral terms, side with the public world against the individual morally. I knew people made great efforts to get good jobs, but I thought it was because they wanted the money or the power. Intelligence, responsibility, values, surely such words applied to the private world, the personal life? I thought Cambridge had implied that.

I realize that I was something of a special case in this, and that those undergraduates who, for instance, spoke of Union debates, however lightly they took them, probably got no shock when they went to the Appointments Board. But I was not unique, and the class to which I belonged is surely the one to which the university owes most; the class whose main job in life will not be the exercise of power but the working out of ideas, and whose theory of social responsibility is wholly the work of their education. This class, I claim, must now be deeply bewildered and lost, socially. The decay of humanism has left the forms of public life, at the university and outside, half-empty monuments, inviting mockery.

For me at least Cambridge, like the world-picture it offered, had been a mass of fragments, held together by a quite accidental framework of humanism; and the fragments that glittered most were the most knife-edged and unusable. They were also extraordinarily few. It happened that a friend of mine set himself to learn a lot of different kinds of knowledge, Greek, philosophy, theology, and more. But it was clear to me that this was a personal eccentricity, that knowing a lot was irrelevant, since the important thing was to see, to feel, to know, to understand, one's own experience, in the way Lawrence, Kafka, Dostoevsky had. I didn't even once go to look at the Cavendish in all those three years. No one ever authoritatively told me I should.

C. P. Snow's theory of the two cultures seems to me to become most irrefutable if one puts it that there is an antagonism between literary people and science; and that along with this, deriving from the same source, goes a provincialism, a contented specialization, on the part of nearly all acute intelligence today. It is from these two together that proceeds the waste of manpower and brainpower which Snow describes.

It is not, as is too commonly lamented, that everybody is blindly enthusiastic about science nowadays, and nobody cares about culture. On the contrary, it seems to me that an overrating of literature (and the arts) is just as prevalent, and even more dangerous, than any general love of science. In Trilling's essay he remarks that for most students the ideas they meet in a modern literature course will be the most important ones of their college career; and that this is because of the agreement, ever growing in assertiveness, that art yields more truth than any other activity. In political matters an embodiment of the personal virtues like George Orwell, a typical figure of modern sensibility, commands our loyalty and love quite in excess of his political wisdom. The noun intellectual has taken on connotations of psychological-moral agony that exclude brilliant scientists, as Snow points out.

It is not the arts that are at a discount, but humanism. People no longer believe in the possibility of putting together the knowledge they find in literature with the knowledge of science and with the events of modern history, and making any important sense of them. They actively and effectively disbelieve in attempts to do that. One of the most striking events of modern cultural history is the complete disappearance of the whole encyclopaedist movement of the Twenties and Thirties. One thinks of Wells's three major compilations, what initial success they had (*An Outline of History* sold a million and a half in America alone and was translated into every language), and what distinguished minds were associated with them – Julian Huxley a co-author of *The Science of Life*, Gilbert Murray and Ernest Barker helping with the history book, Keynes, Laski, Wallas, Kingsley Martin with *The Work, Wealth, and Happiness of Mankind*. Hundreds of thousands of copies must exist still. One imagines them in school libraries; there is certainly no evidence that any educated adult reads them. Educated England completely rejected the responsibility to know and understand the modern world which Wells tried to fix on it.

What Wells was after was not humanism, of course, but encyclopaedism. His educational reforms include universities only as research centres. He was deeply sceptical about art and religion, and rejected in effect the whole personalism of modern literature; the characters of his last novels are created in the same journalistic style as his earliest. He wrote for the man in the street, ignoring the man in the library. But his books and his memory have disappeared not through any act of revenge, but through passive indifference. Educated people have been convinced that their only responsibilities were to their special discipline, and that any attempt to communicate to a wider audience than one's immediate colleagues would be vulgarization. T. S. Eliot had announced that poetry had to be obscure now, and that cultural values had to be created and transmitted by the few; popular poetry came to mean bad poetry. Rutherford had said (when Jeans's *The Mysterious Universe* came out) that if anyone at the Cavendish were thinking of writing a book called *The Mysterious Atom*, he should call in at his (Rutherford's) office before he went to the publisher. Journals like *Scrutiny*, concerned for standards, excoriated the scientific best-seller as well as its literary equivalents. Perhaps these distinctions between the esoteric and the exoteric truths were not more rigid in themselves than those of earlier times, but their effects were more widespread. Because these esoteric truths were not Laputan, or Ivory Tower, but explosive; both brands. Rutherford's work with the atom turned out, within twenty years, and against all his expectations, to be the source of terrible anxiety and fear to every member of the nation. And Eliot's work (along with Kafka's, Lawrence's, etc.) made it impossible for anyone who read it to put any vigorous animal faith in social forms. Both of these effects are more drastic than resulted from esoteric scholarly or artistic truths before.

We need a new humanism, to show how a man can know what Rutherford knew and what Eliot knew, and can become, not despite but because of that knowledge, fully a citizen of our world. We need to break the tabu of incommunicability that has been laid on that knowledge; to learn to transmit it to those with equal though different intellectual experience. The belief that a non-scientist cannot achieve any significant understanding of science must be dismissed as a delusion, a symptom of the disease itself. The difficulties are of course great. But they cannot be insoluble. For the problem is not to acquire a certain amount of information, or even understanding, but to employ a certain amount of serious attention. It is *our* activity, the way we act on our tiny section of physics or chemistry, the depth in us to which we are engaged, not the depth of the science we know, that is important. What we need is intellectual engagement, imaginative participation at the same level of intellect and imagination as we know in our own subject; though nine-tenths of this material must be taken on trust. A good teacher of science can do that in a year starting literally from scratch, just as a good teacher of literature can.

It may not even be necessary to have any new courses, at least at university level. What is essential is that university teachers should be humanists. They must be in some sense committed to the whole scope of modern knowledge as well as to their own subject. Whatever that subject, modern knowledge must include modern literature and modern science. And commitment to it must mean a humanism more sober, more realistic, more convinced, than our supervisor offered us, and less partisan, less partial, less murderous, than Dr Leavis's. It must mean a continuing effort to draw together strands of intellectual activity – strands which do not belong together in most ways – and to make some sense of them.

Such a humanism would not offer us an explanation, much less a solution, of the problems and tensions of modern life. It would offer us a way of talking about and investigating them which would unite all intelligent men, and create a harmony of exerted powers, within which we could know what we need to know, and would save us from hysteria and cynicism and passivity. And it would offer the great universities a meaning they must otherwise disastrously lack.

That is the truth as exactly as I could then, or can now, formulate it; and yet there are perhaps ways it outreaches itself. I certainly did not mean to imply, for instance, that there is no humanism in the world today. Polanyi, Schrodinger, Oppenheimer, Snow, Williams, Trilling, all the people I quote from, to go no further, are humanists by my definition. Indeed, measuring upwards from zero, there can be few people who are not, *in some measure, and in some direction. Cautiously speaking, I should claim no more than that that measure and those directions are inadequate; that we need a very strong and thriving humanism, and we have a rather sickly and patchy affair. But cautious speech would not meet the case. I could present it truthfully only in that more emphatic and positive mode.*

Moreover, one can be a good humanist in some ways while sinning mortally against the faith in others. This is the aspect of the problem to focus on. The evil is that nowadays intellectual virility is so much a matter of these bold sins against humanism, against lax inclusiveness of interests and largeness of tone. It is rare in our day and culture, surely, to find any serenity of voice and breadth of vision which has not cost dear in force and incisiveness. Perhaps it was always rare, but now the rarity is more unfortunate, because we absolutely need to articulate breadth with incisiveness.

One is bound to ask how this theory would apply to countries whose culture is based on, or at least modified by, a principle profoundly different from the equivalent ideas in the West, the principle of Marxism. To answer such a question would require a great deal of work, perhaps another book, but it is worth noting one or two considerations which should form part of any answer. Michael Polanyi, in Personal Knowledge, *makes a good deal of the difference, for the individual's intellectual vitality, between living in a Marxist and in a liberal state today.*

Marxism, says Polanyi, is still intellectually powerful today (despite its rigidities and exaggerations, and despite all those prophecies that time has proved false) because it enables its adherents to indulge the modern mind's two characterizing traits; its inordinate passion for moral righteousness, and its inordinate demand for intellectual objectivity; both of which derive from the belief that all knowledge, all thought, must try to be purely scientific and objective. Thought must *be objective; there is as much heat in the verb as there is ice in the adjective; and that heat of passionate motive stays crudely righteous in Marxism, unmodified by subjective self-criticism. These seemingly antithetical passions dominate the modern mind, and together give it its characteristic tone and drive. They have enfeebled Western liberalism, the effort at objectivity tripping up the moral enthusiasm in, for instance, the intelligent Englishman's faith in his country's foreign policy. But they have given the Marxists double energy. Even Marxism's declared intention to act unscrupulously has a* moral *appeal; it announces superior moral conviction, as well as superior intellectual energy. Why have Western intellectuals gone over to Marxism, despite its threats to their freedom of thought, except because its moral nihilism seemed the proof of moral passion? In a class society material interests are immanent in moral aspirations; in a socialist society the reverse is true; perhaps only a Marxist can swallow the second proposition, but the first is admitted throughout the Western world, because of its 'objectivity', because of our theory of knowledge. This weakens the power to believe of individual liberals, and strengthens the power to believe of individual Marxists, because only a society which shares a faith can make individual faith possible.*

That is convincing, and important. This moral forcefulness, moreover, does affect the problem analysed in my essay. The interests of the state in Marxism have dominated and directed and connected those separatist concerns with pure artistic and pure scientific truth; and there is probably more 'general belief' in Russia than there is in any Western country. But there is plenty of evidence that this is the result not of any immaculate conception of the intellect in a Marxist society, but of a punitive outlawing of certain natural functions of that intellect. This evidence is particularly clear in the field of literature, despite those estimable novels about true hearted right-thinking heroes of the people; not that Russian writers don't really like Communism, but that they would, if they could, express their feelings about it in something much more like the novels of the decadent West.

The Pasternak case showed that this is exactly what the Marxist state will not tolerate. Dr Zhivago *was not anti-communist, but it was anti-political in the sense that its author was concerned with truths of personal experience above all others; it was a Russian example of the modern literary movement. As such, it was not a good communist novel, deserved no enthusiastic praise, deserved rather discouragement. But that case was only the logical result of the whole Soviet policy in literature, its denial of Dostoevsky and Blok, its institutionalization of Gorky. Gorky had five universities named after him, a major city, a publishing house, etc. etc.; and he was institutionalized in an even more significant sense during his lifetime, by his enormous output of plays and novels, essays and autobiographies, and by his busy-ness with reviews, publishing houses, book series, anthologies, translations, libraries. He was called on to speak for the nation, about and to literature.*

Gorky rejected, for Russia, the direction modern literature was taking, and has followed. He rejected Dostoevsky and Andreyev; Mayakovsky rejected Yesenin and Blok. Among Western writers, Gorky was enthusiastic about Wells's novels and dismissed Proust's. He preserved a more than nineteenth-century faith in science, in progress, in industrialization. He believed in man as a part of society; 'It is not about myself I am speaking,' he said in his autobiography, 'but about Russia.' The literary price he paid was made clear by Tolstoy in his comment to Chekhov. 'One may invent anything one pleases, but one cannot invent psychology, and what one finds in Gorky is precisely psychological invention; he describes what he himself has not felt.' That was not a crucial criterion in the age of Milton, but in modern literature it for some reason is, and in consequence very little of Gorky now seems worth reading.

He made himself a great Soviet writer, and by so doing he sacrificed his chance to make himself a great modern writer. The two things are not compatible; the general level of Russian literature shows it, too. If the last thirty years have produced great novels there, then they must be – and the possibility of this hypothesis is an argument for my case – in the form of hidden, secretly written, unread manuscripts. In other words, modern literature obeys the same laws the world over; it can be great only if it is allowed to be free – free to be socially destructive, amongst other things. Marxism has not really solved the problem by creating a morally and socially constructive set of books by prescription.

The story of literature in the Western society has a corresponding but contrary weakness, an over-emphasis on the prophetic and irrational and socially destructive activities of literature. This is perhaps most extreme in the current theories of American literature. In the kind of criticism now written, and in the current interpretations of Hawthorne and Twain (more startling than the misreadings of Faulkner, because so anachronistic), we see the hypertrophy of modern literary intuitions into cultural theories. It is assumed that all free intelligence since the Industrial Revolution must have been intuitively anti-social; that all anti-social intelligences, in fact, must have been keener than the others; and books and authors are grotesquely misread and mis-evaluated in consequence.

Surely it is clear, quite empirically, that both the Russian and the American views are mistaken? Surely it is reasonable to argue that they are both reactions (in opposite directions) to the fact of a modern sensibility so largely anti-humanist, and to which the only useful response must be the search for a newer, more resourceful, more flexible humanism?

4. An Explanatory Lecture

This next chapter is based on a lecture I gave to a university English society. It is an application of the last chapter's thesis to the literary culture, an attempt to show in more detail how and why a literary education today need not make one into a humanist, but, uncounteracted, may well leave one in some imbalance, a little right of centre. ('Right' because of the distrust of social machinery, the primary loyalty to personal relations, though, of course, this can include a 'leftish' radicalism as extreme as you like – Tory anarchy is perhaps the typical literary man's politics.)

It is also a defence of literary training as a general education. That defence is offered as being preliminary to the attack, but it is obviously, as I read it now, more than that. It is a reconsideration and redefinition of my own training in the light of more recent experience in other fields; a re-assertion of all there still was to assert, to hold on to, at this point in the project. I had been in some sense travelling away from that training and those old loyalties. This was the moment to establish the other sense, in which I had been staying where I was, and merely re-defining my position.

The Dangers of a literary education

THE dangers I am concerned with are roughly social; rather than, for instance, religious. It is a threat to our full functioning as social beings, our happy self-respect and self-knowledge in that role, the *social* effects of literary sensibility, that I want to discuss.

My main point is that literary sensibility may have a partly harmful effect. But I come to that conclusion only after, and still without renouncing, my larger belief that literary sensibility is a great help to one's social conscience, a stimulant, a corrective, a refinement, a perfection. That belief is perhaps still somewhat exaggerated in me. I find it hard to believe that anyone can be socially responsible if he has no sensitiveness to language and to literature.

To be sure, therefore, that you come up to my present point from the right direction, and get hold of it from the right angle, and don't wrench it out of its necessary context, I must spend much of my time explaining why I think *that*. But one of the incidents that started me thinking along my present lines may fix my final destination in the reader's mind.

I discovered when I was an undergraduate that I had the habit of using the phrase 'garden-suburb' as a pejorative adjective. Rupert Brooke's garden-suburb poetry, for instance, or 'an innocence which smacks more of the garden suburb than of the Garden of Eden'. E. H. Carr in *What is History?* says historians with no philosophy of history are like nudists in a garden suburb pretending that this is the natural way to dress.

What troubled me was the question, what did I mean by the phrase? I had never been in a garden suburb. I had seen Welwyn Garden City from the train, but plainly I didn't mean anything about that or any actual particular place. I meant something about the general idea and ideal of them. But then why was I using that pejoratively? On the whole, my political views were in favour of the ideal of garden cities; they seemed like honourable solutions to serious problems. No doubt they weren't the perfect solution, but as I knew so little about them, I was in no position to be, I wasn't being, discriminatively critical. My considered, reasoned opinion would have to be that they were on the whole a good thing. Certainly respect-worthy; but I was talking as if they were inherently absurd; not respect-worthy.

To some extent I was doing this just because it was a smart thing to say, a conversational ploy. But not entirely. To some extent I really thought and felt this way. Not so much consciously, and certainly not when I was being politically or socially conscious. But as a result, an indirect result, of certain other quite serious and real interests. That is, the phrase didn't lose its point and sting when I confronted it squarely. Its point and sting were sustained by serious though hidden feelings. And those feelings were, of course, those I got from literature.

From a literary point of view, garden cities are categorically funny. Can one imagine a poem using the phrase except satirically? Can one imagine a serious novel treating it any other way, or anyone from Eliot to Lawrence referring to it respectfully? Even the most politically conscientious of writers, George Orwell, could not manage that. That was why I instinctively spoke of garden suburbs as figures of fun, where life would necessarily be prim, narrow, feeble, cramped, unreal. While at the same time I considered and voted for them as a bold constructive idea which in the right hands could solve some of the problems of a highly industrialized society.

This split was, of course, only typical of a dozen other cases. I found it difficult to read political speeches and pamphlets, because so much of the language seemed either dead or inflated; it so rarely had the kind of interior guarantees of its own honesty and scrupulousness I had learned to look for. I found most statements of social objectives, most descriptions of social ideas, painfully thin and unconvincing – they weren't good representations of life, because so much of the crucial detail, so much of the complexity,[1] was left out. I found most accounts of the machinery of government, local or national, the procedure of committees and elections and juries, irrelevant – to what? To what really mattered, to what life was like, not only for me, but for everyone this machinery was supposed to serve. It made me impatient to hear it described with emotion and excitement. At the same I realized that this impatience was unjustifiable, irresponsible, destructive; I only couldn't get rid of it. But it was not just me or just impatience; it was being fed by the diet I was getting so much from in other ways, my literary education. But why that should be I could not understand.

You can see the same issue in the current quarrel over the two cultures. C. P. Snow in the Rede Lecture claimed that literary

---

[1] Complexity is one of the war-cries of the literary culture. We find most other people, especially those who propose forms of social action, simple-minded. Too often this expresses only the rancour of our own impotent passivity.

people tend to sneer at things like garden suburbs and the practical social idealism they typify. F. R. Leavis in his lecture printed in the *Spectator* afterwards, claimed that the study of literature leads one to the deepest understanding of and response to social problems.

This was a paradox for me because I believed in literary training and literary sensibility as socially useful among other things. Nobody thinks of T. S. Eliot or D. H. Lawrence as model democrats, or of *The Waste Land* or *Women in Love* as being about good citizenship. But both *are* about the impact of modern civilization on the finest, keenest, most intelligent, most serious minds involved in it.

Those are, however, highly complex works of art. We must begin more simply and define our terms. Literary sensibility is a set of aptitudes and habits of response to written language; that set which is not limitedly practical, nor specially political, economic, etc. Limitedly practical meaning that one is reading or listening mostly to acquire information which one will then do something about, in some simple line of endeavour.

Literary sensibility takes note of the way things are said. It notes – to be as objective and specific as possible – the number and nature of the adjectives in a description, the mood, tense, voice, of the verbs in a narrative, the examples in an explanation, the objections foreseen and answered or avoided in an argument, the images, the metaphors, the alliteration, the allusions, in a poem. It notes all this while following the argument or seeing the thing described, and this notation is the more important part of its activity. Because these details are the literary data it interprets; they become when interpreted the literary behaviour it evaluates. By that behaviour, as much as by his statements, it judges a writer's intelligence and maturity and originality.

From these details, for instance, it deduces the relationship the writer wants setting up between himself and the things described or discussed; whether he uses the first or third person, whether he claims to know everything about the matter or nothing. It deduces, and obediently constructs, the relationship the writer wants with his readers; whether he pretends we aren't there, or pretends we're old friends, whether he in effect preaches to us, confesses, chats, or drawls.

Literary sensibility follows his directions in all such things, estimates them as it does so, and responds accordingly. The response is the key point. The reader does not only say, 'I understand; I see that this writer uses the third person, and affects omniscience, and makes the reader feel naïve.' Nor does he only estimate this behaviour: 'This effect is skilfully contrived, and deserves high literary praise.' Beyond this, the reader responds; saying something like, 'This man has the right to ask me to believe what he says and see what he describes and feel what he dramatizes. To see, to feel, to believe, angrily or lovingly or however it is he asks me to respond; above all, obediently and unprotectedly. He has the right to make me, for instance, imagine myself present at a child-murder, or to go through the death of Ivan Ilyich, or – a different sort of case – to ponder the minutiae of some quite trivial social manners.'

Not that all writers ask us to do things we resist or suspect. But they all ask us to perform some imaginative feat, however easy, natural, unnoticeable it may be, and our only ultimate warrant for obeying them is that we know they have the right to command our feelings. Most we must refuse to respond to deeply. For we, each one of us, grant a man that right over our imagination as we see fit. The excitement we have when we read *King Lear* is derived in a sense not from Shakespeare at all. It is most profoundly derived from (a) our own imaginations, and (b) the common vivid facts of growing old and losing power. Shakespeare connects our imaginations with those facts. He doesn't tell us things we didn't know. The daily newspaper offers us similar stimulus to pity and terror at the human condition. Shakespeare merely persuades us to feel what we could feel by ourselves if we weren't too lazy, too stupid, too self-protective. But self-protection is necessary and justified because so many people try to play on our feelings for wrong or inadequate reasons. We must lower that sceptical critical guard over our feelings only when we are persuaded of the writer's rights. Shakespeare's greatness as a writer consists in that very complete persuasion.

How does he persuade us? By the presentation of those purely literary data we then interpret, and the performance of that literary behaviour we then evaluate. But this does not mean just by being skilful. Literary skill (understood in any limited sense) does not constitute a right to command the reader's imagination. You can be quite a fine craftsman without being an artist at all, and the difference is that only an artist persuades the reader to let him tap any of the multitudinous sources of pure feeling, whose circulation deep within us constitutes our imagination; whose innermost sacred responsiveness, engageability, plasticity, constitutes our soul. Because the artist shows – in and through those literary skills – intelligence about life, understanding and experience of, passionate concern for, beliefs and feelings and relationships. Graham Greene's skill, in matters of narrative, let's say, is often remarkable; George Eliot's is often not. But what George Eliot does, and Graham Greene does not, is to persuade us to respond to her themes, to yield up our self-protective resistances. We, each one of us, judge the writer's intelligence, understanding, imaginative authority, on the evidence of the way he writes, and, if he passes every test, let ourselves respond to every subtlety as he directs, and even with the big overwhelming feelings.

That is why in literature the way a thing is said is more important than what is said. Because it is only if we are persuaded to trust the writer that what is said becomes real at all. Obviously it is Romeo and Juliet dying we are moved by, not skilful verse-writing, but we would not be moved by that story at all if it were told by another writer. The skill, by demonstrating intelligence about life, has won our attentiveness, our responsiveness – our belief. Imaginative literature is that kind in which the reality is totally dependent on the writer. In a book of political history, or even a political novel (take Arthur Koestler's *Darkness at Noon*) some of the reality is independent of the author. We respond to the story of Russian Communism attentively because of its intrinsic interest. It is important because these things happened. Romeo and Juliet never happened. Only Shakespeare (with our consent) makes them happen in us, and (with our consent) makes us delight in love-and-death.

When I talk of consent, or of our granting an author the right to make us feel something, I am describing from another point of view what is more often called his successful evocation of that something. For instance, in the case of the Alpine scenery described at the end of *Women in Love*, a classic case of successful writing, critics usually say that Lawrence makes us see the mountains. My point is that we *try* to see whatever he names because he has convinced us of his authority in this matter; convinced us that he has seen *these* mountains, but also that he knows about natural beauty of all kinds and about the whole morality of the aesthetic life, so that we are ready to follow his every hint implicitly and passionately, to feel, in fact, more than we would if we actually saw the mountains themselves. So that if Lawrence says, 'the snowy peak was rosy in the evening light', we are ready to imagine that, and respond to it as beautiful and significant, while in another novelist exactly the same words would leave us quite unmoved. Those words are *not* in themselves remarkable. But I have granted Lawrence the right to evoke such feelings in my mind; I work with him to discover and arouse those feelings.

Most of the time Lawrence keeps redeeming that right by finding words and details that are brilliant in themselves; so that one can describe what happens as skilful writing on his part, with our part reduced to passive (even if critical) reacting. In the case I cite, however, it surely becomes clear that we co-operate actively, and that the brilliant details merely guide us. So there are three acts in the process of reading; skill and intelligence recognized, inner submission in the degree they deserve, response in the degree we submit.[1] One proof of that is our very limited response to quite vivid phrasing in Graham Greene, or in Poe, who might quite well strike off a better single phrase than the one I quoted. Another proof is that in the wrong mood we can remain unmoved by the finest passages; because we need to co-operate actively. Another is our specially full, deep response to books which we

[1] I don't mean that the act of submission is total or final. The reader remains a critic. He is always defining those areas in which Lawrence is an *un*trustworthy guide. But in those areas in which he is trustworthy one is critical only in the somewhat paradoxical sense of appreciative dependence and enthusiastic discipleship.

know from re-reading deserve our co-operation; the first reading of especially a contemporary book does not give most people an equally satisfying experience, because they have not opened the protective locks in their channels of feeling.[1]

My point is that the reader's activity, in grasping the sentence in front of him, is equally intellectual and moral. One must inter- pret and estimate the writer's abilities, intentions, authority, but that estimate leads to, *is*, a yielding of power over one's own imagination to this writer – a yielding to this chosen individual of (limited) directive power over the sources of one's own conscience, sensibility, interests, and habits of mind. ('Yielding' is perhaps too feminine, for one acts, one co-operates, one imagines for oneself, boldly.) This is the inner drama of the act of reading, and on this is based the pride of the student of literature. It is not so much the material he works on, the great heritage of poetry, drama, fiction, nor even the values he finds there, the treasury of tradition, imagination, intelligence; it is the action he performs on that material and on contemporary literature which gives him so strong a sense of intellectual virtue. He feels himself the protagonist of all humanistic values. Believing in this is what gave me the sense that my literary education could not be at odds with, in opposition to, any important responsibility. I think now, looking back, that in this so-strong feeling lay the danger; because if you identify this one intellectual discipline, the art of reading, with moral discipline, you are in danger of not recognizing the moral content of other kinds of intellectual work. That is, if you are enthusiastic in your identification. The work *you* do for the imagination and for moral values (personal and general) seems more central, more radical, more strenuous than anybody else's.

Our definition of literary sensibility included habits of response. For these are aptitudes realized and developed and trained. Habits change; literary habits change with the literature of the

---

[1] The worst misunderstanding of the word criticism is to think of it as procedures for the inhibition of feeling; in fact, it only guards and trains our feelings, and will in fact deliver them to the right writer much more naked, sensitive, and full, than they come in the unthinking untrained response.

day; and literary sensibility is a different thing now from what it was in the nineteenth century. It is the same thing, because it is the same aptitude; but it is different, because it has different habits. It looks out for, primarily, and responds to, primarily, different things. We don't, in poetry, look out for and value mellifluousness as the Victorians did. We don't, in fiction, look out for and value the big tear-jerking scene as they did.

What has the modern sensibility looked out for? The use of myth and symbol, energy and eccentricity of expression, sexual explicitness, irony of tone, anger, rebellion against conventional attitudes, a frank use of ugliness, obscurity of style and recklessness of opinion. You see all this in the great modern literary figures, Lawrence, Dostoevsky, Proust, and Joyce.

Two things characterize these writers, distinguish them from those of the past. The first is that they are not 'literary'. If you actually read them you cannot talk about them as ornaments to gracious living. You should not talk about Jane Austen as if she were, but you can. You cannot talk like that about Dostoevsky. You should not talk about Fielding as a literary extension to your club-life, but you can; you can't talk about Lawrence that way. Because these modern writers are anti-humanist in effect. They make a savage criticism of all the social bonds, all the contracts men enter into to relieve themselves of personal loneliness, or to create a corporate consciousness. They make nonsense of those social bonds; Proust and Lawrence, so different in every other way, are alike in that. Not that Jane Austen and Fielding were propagandists for society. They had sharp criticisms to make. But they were not basically anti-humanist.

The second point is that these writers investigate the question of how a human being should live with a reckless passion which Jane Austen and Fielding would have thought unsuitable. Because in the eighteenth century a writer was not supposed to be a priest of personal freedom. But Dostoevsky, Kafka, Lawrence, were all just that. And consequently the whole study of literature today is permeated with that concern. It is the critic's concern as well as the writer's. Leavis, for instance, attacking Snow, says,

In coming to terms with great literature we discover what at bottom we really believe. What for – what ultimately for? What do men live by – the questions work and tell at what I can only call a religious depth of feeling. Perhaps, with my eye on the adjective, I may just recall for you Tom Brangwen, in *The Rainbow*, watching by the fold in lambing time under the night sky: 'He knew he did not belong to himself.'

Leavis's attack on mass civilization, and even much of his best criticism, reminds one of Kierkegaard's preaching, not only in its direction but in its arguments, and even more in its temper. There are whole excerpts from *Purity of Heart is to Will One Thing* which could be made to fit indistinguishably into some of Leavis's essays. And where we disagree with him – over Conrad and Hawthorne, notably – it is often because he is reading a great lesson in spirituality into an inadequate text. Such disagreement, even when radical, affects our loyalty very little; because it does not affect his status as prophet, which is the crucial thing.

Those then are the two points about modern literature and modern literary sensibility relevant to this argument, the anti-social character and the religious strain. From them derive the passionate, near-metaphysical morality, the anger and irony, the distrust of material progress, the rebellion against all conventional standards, the distrust of human nature itself in its more organized manifestations. These are all part of literary sensibility today.

And what do we mean by society when we speak of the social role of literary sensibility? We mean co-operative efforts to live together, to create and run institutions, to dispense justice and guarantee freedom, to earn a living and defend one's country, to preach and practise a religion, etc. All the things men do together, as a result of living together. And the social role of literary sensibility is its application to all this. But social does not include heart-to-heart talks, or friendships or marriage, or country walks, or behaviour at parties, or sense of humour, or religious meditations, all of which are to be categorized as personal. About that category we need say no more, for the time being. It is clear how centrally important to a novelist all *such* material is – how literary sensibility helps one grasp and evaluate such material in one's own life, too.

But how does literary sensibility apply to the facts of society? How, to put the thing at its crudest, does it help one as a citizen, to create and run institutions, etc.?

Briefly, then, sensitiveness to language applies itself to the leaders of our society and their manifestoes. To the politicians, priests, teachers, employers, trade-union chairmen, and their speeches, pamphlets, advertisements. Language is, at the least, one of the most important modes of expression a man has; conscious and unconscious expression; and if you can read that you can judge him. You can judge his logic, his quickness of mind, his honesty, his subtlety, his loyalties, his literacy. Even when he thinks he is protecting himself, this is announced in the way he talks. Take, for instance, what Leavis finds of Snow's personality in *The Two Cultures*; things Snow certainly did not intend to reveal. A reader may be wrong in such an interpretation – as I think Leavis is in this case – but he is right to attempt it; a man's language can tell us every bit as much as Leavis claims to find there, and so our literary sensibility can be an organ of practical judgement.

Secondly, literary sensibility fosters a concern for culture as a whole. Literature is a co-operative venture. It is not a series of isolated books and isolated readers. Few good books have been written without a highly specified group of readers in mind. No high standards have ever been maintained unless that group was intelligent and informed; was, in fact, a more or less organized and vocal public, expressing its reactions, guided by good critics. You don't get far in the study of literature before you realize that.

Then literary sensibility leads one to a concern for education. Taste and culture are after all primarily matters of what one knows, and the way one knows it – the feelings one has about the things known. So also are bad taste and bad culture which are propagated by various commercial media of communication; and the schools and universities must take on the task of combating them which was formerly left to less institutional guardians. Dr Leavis's disciples have been the major examples in our time of the responsibility for education derived from a training in literature. We need only mention names like Boris Ford, who edited the

Penguin History of English Literature, and who works at the Institute of Education at Sheffield; William Walsh, who is Professor of Education at Leeds, and whose book, *Literature and Education*, reveals him essentially a literary critic; G. H. Bantock, who wrote *Freedom and Authority in Education*; David Holbrook, who wrote *English for Maturity*; etc.

Fourthly – this may sound a little vaguer – literary sensibility leads one to a concern for the whole life of an individual in society, and so to a responsibility for that society and the conditions it offers. Here we can think of Richard Hoggart's *Uses of Literacy* and Raymond Williams's *Culture and Society*. We can also return, at this level of complexity, to *The Waste Land* and *Women in Love*. These are all concerned with the quality of life our society makes possible to its members; and that, too, is what Leavis and Snow disagree over. What will such a phrase mean in the most concrete terms? The simplest kinds of case will be books like *The Road to Wigan Pier* or *Homage to Catalonia*; a determination to tell political truth, an opposition to brutalizing kinds of labour, an effort even to make public libraries places where people want to go. One sees in both Orwell's books how naturally this is allied with a concern for more subtle kinds of truth – about ideas and feelings.

Lastly, and this may be a rather different kind of point, it leads one to a constant concern for the personal; distinguishing the person from the group, but also from the individual. As an individual, a man exemplifies general rules. As a person, he is unique. As an individual, he belongs to the class that have blue eyes, the class that have brown hair, the class that have black-rimmed glasses, etc. If you look at him as a person, you see in his face that conjunction of features and expressions which is nowhere else reproduced, and which is full of his self, him. It is clear already in what sense literature is concerned with the person, and non-literature – the tax form or passport – with the individual. Not that a novel cannot also describe individuals; but at its centre will be persons.

But we must go one step further. What is it that makes a face unique? It is not merely the combination of so many categories that you are unlikely to find anybody else with exactly the same proportions, colouring, skin-type; you would still be separate persons, obviously. The uniqueness of a person is a matter of his autonomy. He chooses for himself when to and how to react; so that even if he chose to do it exactly as somebody else did, he would still be unique, because he chose.

Because literature always, essentially, deals with persons, and personality is essentially a matter of freedom, the modern novel is more literary than anything in the past; for it is obsessed with freedom in that sense. In Lawrence's novels everything that happens to a character happens because of his desire, his responsibility, his personality. His physical and accidental individuality is diminished almost to nothing. George Eliot and Tolstoy had a lot to say about personal freedom, but Dostoevsky and Lawrence had everything to say about it. That is the key to modern literature and to the modern sensibility. Leavis, attacking Snow, talks of 'the truth that only in living individuals is life there, and individual lives cannot be aggregated or equated or dealt with quantitatively in any way'. And in another place, 'What is the social hope that transcends, cancels or makes indifferent the inescapable tragic condition of each individual? Where, if not in individuals, is what is to be hoped for to be located?' Again we think of Kierkegaard. Literary criticism and spiritual prophecy are today two branches of the same tree.

Literary training should therefore make one always aware of the persons involved in social and political events, however statistically they may be represented. One should be instinctively aware of other modes of being, even when these others are also a social problem – O.A.S. or juvenile delinquents, the mentally sick, the very old, Fascists, or Mau Mau. And because one is sensitive to the question of personal freedom, one retains a scepticism about political and economic remedies. One doesn't expect simple gratitude when people are finally granted the vote or the rise in pay they have long demanded; one doesn't expect them to be happy or to love one. They are persons. There are ten thousand other factors affecting their reactions, and above all they are free. They can choose how they react. This means you understand your opponents, which complicates your political life, but enriches it.

This surely is the greatest gift of modern literary sensibility to social thought.

For these reasons, therefore, the man with literary training especially today does not feel himself limited to literature; he feels himself the protagonist of the intellectual life in just that noblest phase where it is equally the moral and the imaginative life, that mode of thought which is closest to the pulse of life itself, in the individual and in his society as a whole. How, then, can there be an opposition between that training and any kind of social responsibility?

The only evidence I have so far offered that there is, is that anecdote about the garden suburb. But when I talked of a literary concern for the whole life of an individual leading one to reform public libraries, perhaps you reflected that it doesn't often work out like that. Certainly we all know people with real literary taste, and highly intelligent, who are not at all socially responsible. Often their social irresponsibility seems to be correlated with their literary sensibility. Or at least the unsatisfactory nature of their performance as members of a community seems to have something to do with their strong feeling for literature.

There are those, for instance, who are too sensitive to cope with the world in its grosser aspects. This group includes people we must all respect, people with remarkable talent, and with at least as much seriousness about life as ourselves. It includes, for instance, Virginia Woolf. We must, it is clear, respect such people as well as their suffering; and I think we must admit some connection between that suffering and their talent as writers. One cannot, of course, admire this incapacitation for so much of life. But can one deny that it is in some sense literary? That a great many writers, and intelligent readers, and the literary part of oneself, are, in fact, similarly debilitated? That part of us feels that all life ought to be governed by the values that govern literature, and all experience controlled by the techniques that control the artist's material. We feel that, but, of course, we distrust and rebuke and contradict the feeling.

Then there are those people in whom sensibility manifests

itself socially by a defiant affectation. I suppose the classic cases are people like Oscar Wilde, Tennessee Williams, Truman Capote. It may be too paradoxical to call this group more socially responsible than the last, but one can argue that they are doing something about the fact that they are members of a society. They are enacting a gesture of self-assertion which is an emancipation for other timider people.

But the affected are usually irresponsible, even destructive, over nine-tenths of the area of social life. Their one brave gesture, on behalf of personal freedom, only throws into relief their general self-indulgence. More seriously eccentric writers do discuss the crucial social problems, but in their own idiom; people like Yeats, or Norman Mailer, or Faulkner. It is difficult for economists or sociologists to recognize their own subjects when they emerge from the hands of these writers, but there is no doubt the latter are defining important truths as they see them. However, their useful insights are generally bought at the price of much more that is not useful, that is merely mystifying or even pernicious.

Then there are those who use more intelligible language about social problems, but can rest only in extremist positions. The most current example is James Baldwin; others are Sartre and Camus; writers who take their social responsibilities seriously, who even take some part in politics, but whose policies are violently Marxist or Existentialist or at some other extreme. Their policies too often involve sacrificing half the structure of human society, especially the literary-personal half; and have a persistent flavour both of intellectual virtuosity and of emotional hysteria.

More common in England is the kind of intellectuals' conservatism found in T. S. Eliot or Evelyn Waugh. Abroad you find the same phenomenon in Thomas Mann and in Dostoevsky. This derives from a deep intuition of the sources of evil in the individual and of disorder in society; a deep conviction of the need for stability and order at almost any price; a deep scepticism about social and economic reform. Here we have a kind of social responsibility and a typical literary man's politics. We must respect it, but we can hardly get enthusiastic about it. We are bound to feel that the intellectual consistency and moral weight have been bought too dearly; at the expense, too often, of these writers' better feelings and freer intelligence.

Finally, there is the treatment of social problems which translates them all into allegories of personal experience. The great example of this is D. H. Lawrence or Conrad in a novel like *Nostromo*, where the political parties, the foreign policies, the party programmes, etc., are all simplified down till they express personalities or moods, some person's state of soul. Once you do this, once you regard, say, the Conservative Party's policy as expressing a conservative mood, a conservative temperament, a mode of personal reaction to the world around us, then it is easy to discuss politics in literary terms. And of course the Conservative Party is a group of conservative men. But it is also a political entity and has to be understood as that. In fact, it is primarily a political entity and must be understood primarily as that. In so far as you can treat politics as a direct translation of personal moods and intuitions into policies and law, Lawrence and Conrad are brilliant. But you can't go even half-way towards understanding politics along that route. Their treatment of social problems, like all the others, is radically unsatisfying.

But why should literary sensibility, seeming to promise so much in the way of social insight, in fact quite habitually go together with immaturity, evasiveness, incapacitation, of one kind or another? We can't, after all, dismiss the evidence of so many examples as being in each case merely the result of an individual quirk of temperament.

The reasoning we followed before, which seemed to lead in the opposite direction, referred, of course, to a radically limited social interest. The educational-social work of Leavis's disciples has stopped short of properly political issues, kept clear of institutional questions, limited itself to a defence of cultural values (located largely in the realm of the aesthetic or pseudo-aesthetic) against the pressures of contemporary civilization; of the pseudo-scientific and the commercial and the mass-produced. It is also the work of one group of teachers of English; we can admire it, while regarding it as in some sense abnormal. We certainly cannot take it as typically literary when we weigh against it the behaviour not only of other academics but even more of writers; including the writers they themselves most admire.

So we look for some explanation, some idea that links together what we have observed from outside of writers' behaviour with what we have reasoned more deductively from within our reading. Why, despite all our reasoning, we must not look to literary men for social wisdom. Why we must, in fact, check and counter-balance, counteract, our literary sensibility, when we consider social problems.

The answer seems to me to be that the human being in society is not fully a person. The literary mind, so beautifully adept in appreciating persons, can also handle individuals, so long as there are not too many of them, but is very ill equipped to deal with groups. Of course, this is a simplification. A novelist can *present* a group; a crowd or an institution. He can include it in his canvas; but as a horizon. The moment a group begins to act as a group, and its individual members cease to be persons, that moment a novelist has reached the limit of his scope. He cannot stay there; he has to return from it to his central terrain of persons acting on each other.[1]

But society does not consist primarily of persons, free entities creating their own destinies by acts of choice largely in the realm of personal relations. It consists of individuals, and even more importantly of groups. This is also a simplification, perhaps. We remain persons, even in our social combinations. This causes much of the complexity, and more of the interest. But nobody needs reminding of that. What they may need reminding of – what I at least needed reminding of – is that it is equally a simpli-fication and a falsification to say that society consists of persons. That sounds more plausible; it is what all literary people, perhaps all literate people, habitually say; because we assume that 'person' includes all 'individual' contains and more. But surely the

---

[1] I am talking of the *modern serious* novel. Is it not a good deal because Snow does deal with institutions, and with people as members of them, that his novels offend so many people aesthetically, that Dr Leavis insists that Snow does not know what a novel is, does not begin to be a novelist?

idea of a person in fact excludes or diminishes or at least depreciates the impersonal, material, accidental aspects of a human being, the facts of his group life? The fact that all the time, to some extent, you think and act largely according to categories, as an Englishman, a schoolteacher, a conscript, a taxpayer; that your thought and action along those lines, though not sharply personal, is important to you, and difficult for you, and dignified in you.

Leavis, arguing with Snow, quotes from *Women in Love*, 'I want every man to have his share in the world's goods, so that I am rid of his importunity, so that I can tell him: "Now you've got what you want – you've got your fair share of the world's gear. Now, you one-mouthed fool, mind yourself and don't obstruct me." ' This is, in fact, a typical literary view. I have every sympathy with it – too much sympathy – but I must insist that it allows politics, economics, etc., very little dignity. All the excitement and richness of life is made personal; society is made merely a minor and mechanical function.

That is why there is a strain of protest in most literary men's comments on social problems. If you think of society as made up of persons, then social thought does not make sense. It is not only that all the wrong categories are used. It is that *no one* can grasp the idea of 100,000 or 1,000,000 persons. The essence of a person is his uniqueness, his uncategorizableness, as Leavis insisted.

Of course, we all, even the most literary minds, do think of people as individuals, and in categories, to some extent. But if we are literary we take less interest in them; we think less keenly about them. We cannot take seriously other people's thinking along these lines. Because a person who can be put wholly into a category is not interesting, not fully alive. And when they are wholly members of a group we lose interest even more. They have lost all that freedom and personality that interested us; and if they acquire a new kind of power and activity – a kind of inverse freedom – as a result of belonging to the group, we regard that with suspicion and alarm. Hence the poverty of experience and hysteria of tone we find in literary pronouncements on social problems.

And hence – to return to my beginning – my undergraduate

remark about garden suburbs. That remark, the tone of which I
picked up so instinctively from my reading, betrays an impatience
with, a hostility to, social and political idealism. It betrays an
indifference to the fact of a garden suburb and a hostility to the
ideal. This hostility and indifference, this impatience and irre-
verence, were, as I told you before, quite unconscious. They
contradicted my conscious ideas. Where did they come from?
From my gradual indoctrination with the primacy of the person,
and the insignificance of the less personal parts of a human being.
No free rich personality is going to find salvation in a garden
suburb; and from a literary point of view such salvation is the only
thing that deserves excitement; what the suburb offers as a good
life is so irrelevant to that question it seems absurd. My sneer
came from the success of my literary education.

That, then, is my proposition; that there is a danger inherent
in the success of a modern literary education. It is not only that
this education concentrates attention on certain features of life
at the expense of others – all effective modes of education do that;
but ours intoxicates us into feeling we need nothing more.

*That essay seems to me a defence of the literary education quite as much as
an attack on it. But to other people it has seemed that, in this book as a
whole, I have wanted to punish only the literary half of this joint and
reciprocal failure, this complex crisis. I hope that is not true, and that I
have merely begun my argument with an assumption of general agreement
which is nearer to my critics' own position than they realize. I have taken
for granted all sorts of general propositions about the inordinate power of
science, all sorts of warnings against it. That, as Mary Hesse puts it in*
Science and the Human Imagination, *the great mass of people in
the Western world live philosophically by a creed – a kind of sensual
empiricism – which was created for and by science. That, in Polanyi's
words, 'Mathematical science is widely accepted as the most perfect of the
sciences, and science as the most perfect of all feats of the intelligence.'
This (everything thus referred to) is indeed the largest single fact about
the modern mind, the grossest single distortion of the modern consciousness.
The literary mind's worst mistakes and distortions are quite secondary to
that; they are defensive reactions against it, as we see in Dostoevsky and*

Lawrence, for instance, and they affect fewer people. But it is quite possible, indeed it is usual, for highly intelligent people to live wholly within a literary enclave, so far as their imaginations go, ruled by those defensive distortions. It is surely quite inadequate to think, 'We live in a scientific age. So we should be anti-scientific.' But isn't this a fair description of much literary apologetics?

There genuinely is, it's true, a crude scientism still abroad in the world. My 'assumption of general agreement' must not be taken to deny the existence of scientism, only its currency among those engaged in this debate. 'Who can doubt that the central scientific problem of our time is the problem of emotion?' asked Howard S. Liddell, director of the Behaviour Farm Laboratory at Cornell. And what he implied is exactly what is made explicit in this passage from Pavlov: 'Only science, exact science about human nature itself, and the most sincere approach to it by the aid of the omnipotent scientific method, will deliver man from his present gloom, and will purge him from his contemporary shame in the sphere of interhuman relationships.' They really thought they could clear up the problems of personal relationships by the use of the 'omnipotent scientific method'. But those remarks were made over a quarter of a century ago, and men of equivalent scientific intelligence rarely talk like that today. There is a continuing enthusiasm for scientific possibility, which offends many literary people, but that is not necessarily crude. There is a continuing crudity among the second- and third-rate intelligences, but they are not to be taken to represent science. Intelligent scientists are no more 'optimistic' than other people today.

A quarter of a century ago they were, perhaps. And it is hard to believe that such optimism did not derive from a culpable innocence. 'When I compare our present knowledge of the workings of the body, and our powers of interfering with and controlling those workings for the benefit of humanity, with the ignorance and despairing impotence of my student days, I feel that I have had the good fortune to see the sun rise on a darkened world.' This was said by Ernest Sparling, the physiologist famous for his work on hormones. It was said in 1923, the year of Antic Hay *(with its famous portrait of a naïve physiologist) at the height of the post-war disillusionment. He added that what he had lived through was not just another renaissance, 'but a new birth of man's powers over his environment and his destinies unparalleled in the whole history of mankind'. A culpable inno-*

cence, no doubt; and yet this clarity of conviction is surely one of the things that feeds that personal decency the most chauvinist literary man is forced to grant to young scientists – to attribute to them rather than to his colleagues as a habitual trait. Our greater awareness seems to cost us too much; in fact, of course, ours is better defined as a different awareness, perhaps equally limited.

It is true also, and more disturbing, that a great deal more money is spent by the modern state on scientific training than on literary; and that there is a very dismaying link between science and militarism. President Eisenhower reminded America of that in his farewell address in 1961. At that time, according to the New York Times, *the Federal Government subsidized 60 per cent of America's total research, and four-fifths of that expenditure went on national defence projects. Nearly 50 per cent of all scientific research was therefore devoted to military purposes. (Nearly 60 per cent of the American budget as a whole was then being spent on defence.) M.I.T. was in the top class (of fifty) of the nation's military contractors. There was, moreover, increasing cross-fertilization between military, industrial, and scientific organizations; leaders in one type of organization were increasingly seconded to another. Seven hundred and twenty-six former top-ranking military officers were then employed by America's leading military contractors. Those military contractors in turn virtually financed the organizations that do the lobbying for the services in Washington. And researchers from university laboratories moved straight across into those same firms. These are three continents of one world, and increasingly interconnected. The literary man never enters that world. The research scientist finds himself in contexts of power, and sometimes in positions of power, utterly alien to the research scholar in literature.*

This interrelationship is obvious when you look at the advertisements in The Scientific American. *Intellectual (scientific) ability is at least asked for by all the big firms that advertise for staff ('Where Ideas Unlock the Future') and the literary man is immediately made conscious of how socially unwanted his own abilities are. Those future-unlocking ideas will not, of course, be what* we *have to offer in the way of ideas. And in half those firms the work done is quite directly related to what they call 'defence'.*

There is every reason to be frightened of the power of science; both as the rival of the arts, and as the arbiter of all our destinies (not the judge but the executioner). Indeed, it is a perfectly rational position to say that if one were given the chance, one would choose to cancel out the mechanical and scientific developments of the last hundred and fifty years. Weighing the advantages against the terrible new risks, I think that most of us would make that choice. But that choice does not exist, and what is not rational is to build an attitude to the modern world on such a base; to face the contemporary and future world mainly with the wish that it had never happened, or rather with resentments, accusations, despairs, self-disengagements, which derive from that wish.

Again, literature perhaps must *take up a defensive position against other educational disciplines. That is perhaps necessary and reasonable. But there is no reason to arrogate to ourselves the prestige of all culture and true humanism. That is not ours. Science, too, is the nexus, for intelligent people, of a whole range of interests, inspirations, disciplines, and other modes of apprehension. You need go no further than those same advertisements in* The Scientific American *for proof of how humour, idealism, common sense, and so on blend in the service of science as much as in the service of literature. 'The pattern of enthusiasm for the tunnel diode coincides curiously with the shape of the characteristic N-curve of the diode itself. Interest among computer engineers quickly rose to a peak, almost as quickly dropped away, and is again on the rise. The reason is obvious. Many of the problems which arose in the early development of high-speed tunnel diode circuitry have been overcome, and practical applications are increasing. Take the work of the Bendix Digital Research Group.' Surely one would rather read that than any advertisement for a literary man's job I know. Or compare just the vocabulary-colour in 'to pot and encapsulate electronic devices . . . resistance to ageing, weathering, flame, ozone, and corona', with the* New Yorker's *'invisibly misted with luminous dew-lit allure'. I don't offer the Elizabeth Arden phrases as a fair representative of the literary mind, but I do as a fair contrast to the* Scientific American *phrases. In many ways science has made a better bargain with commerce and industry in our culture than the humanities have.*

Many literary people just don't know, I think, the ways in which scientific knowledge does *contribute to such 'human' perceptions and qualities – humour, idealism, common sense – does form the nucleus of a sensibility. They insist on those crudities of general thought which could only be fairly associated with science twenty-five years ago, even as a caricature. One glimpse of the opposite truth came for me in J. G. Crowther's account of his tour of the Kremlin in* Industry and Education in Soviet Russia. *In the museum he saw series of '. . . drinking-vessels of the medieval Tsars, which became smaller as the centuries passed and technique advanced so that vintners learned how to increase the alcoholic content of wine and enable a smaller quantity to produce an equal effect'. It is a common-sense deduction which I think would not have occurred to me, just because my training was literary (I would have thought the change was a move-ment in the history of aesthetic taste); and which not only throws a nice ironic light on the sequence of goblets, but also compresses a whole range of human history into manageable size. It is the technologist's joke – it belongs clearly on that side of the cultural divide – but it is just as clearly the intelligent man's joke. This is the aspect of technology literary people should be showing each other, it seems to me, not the inhuman monster which justifies all their heroic hostility. Hostility to science, or to 'an age dominated by science', cannot any way serve the cause of the humanities, or the intelligence of the students to whom it is expounded. It is a form of stupidity, which teachers of literature everywhere should be actively stamping out. There was no room here for even those just criticisms which are already all too current among this book's likely readers.*

5. A particular case

The year 1962-3 I spent teaching at a College of Advanced Technology in the Department of English and Liberal Studies and this next essay derives from that experience. Its form is rather jagged, incorporating a reversal, because the experiment it reports did, too. They both struck on a paradox, an antinomy, an unavoidable discord. The English teacher goes to such a job eager to offer the other culture the benefits of a literary education, in some measure, some fraction; and is gradually forced to admit that those benefits are not wanted; that they are not what is most necessary. Under the present conditions of work, that is, the English teacher cannot give CAT students any significant fraction of an education; less, I think, than the history teacher can. Even when he feels himself specially called to man this particular cultural bridgehead.

This is just another of the paradoxes engendered by the two cultures conflict. The distance between the English teacher and the CAT teacher – in the kind of intellectual work the two practise and understand – has become too great to be bridged under the conditions of work given; and it is no help if the teacher's involuntary missionariness, even when tempered with some acquired modesty about the position of his own discipline, drives him to greater efforts, to works of supererogation. Of course, the problem is not insoluble in practice by some sort of compromise; indeed, some teachers solve it with no sense of strain; but it remains a problem, really marring the act of teaching.

Perhaps I should add that my idea of what Liberal Studies would be before I began teaching them was based on my American experience with Freshman Composition, and other courses which can be described so as to sound very similar. But what, at the CAT, was so significantly called English and Liberal Studies, is in America in effect English as a Liberal Study. There students are made to read arguments, confessions, descriptions, *analyses of experience, by masters of sophisticated language, and then must attempt something similar themselves. What makes it impossible to do that in CATs is not the students, for they seem very similar to freshmen in American state universities, but the conditions of work. There I saw the students three times a week, and before each time they had done some reading; once a week they did some writing; once a fortnight I saw them individually about their writing. With such a scheme it is possible to begin a literary education for quite unliterary students. Should we not therefore press for a similar scheme in this country? I am not sure. First because we could not follow it up properly; even in American universities, with their distribution requirements, this happens only to English majors at best; to attempt it at English CATs would mean to make a wholly unrealistic demand on the students' time. Secondly because, as I say in the essay, few of the English teachers we have at present are trained to deal with students so categorically from the other culture.*

Liberal studies

EDUCATION in England is in the process of acquiring a new category, Liberal Studies; which means the non-professional subjects taken by students at technical colleges, CATs, colleges of art, and so on. An Association for Liberal Education was founded in 1961, which began a journal called *Liberal Education* in 1962, and conferences of Liberal Studies teachers and surveys of Liberal Studies students are nowadays rife. This category is in the process of defining itself, amid the usual turmoil. Policies are being shaped, new jobs are being created, future power is being assigned; there is naturally some jockeying for position. There are also sharp differences of genuine opinion, most of which group themselves around the quarrel between the 'British' and the 'American' interpretations of the phrase. The former wants to give the students something like (within the limits prescribed by their previous preparation and present allocation of time) a university training in history and philosophy and literature. The latter wants to find out from the students (by means of questionnaires and consultations and class discussions) which topic of current interest, or problem of growing up, or useful social skill, they would like to concentrate on that term. I exaggerate both alternatives, of course; or rather, I choose the proposals of the extremists on both sides; most people want something midway, but they feel the tension of being between those two poles. This is an important quarrel, and one cannot pretend to stand above it; I myself belong on the 'British' side; but it is a quite different one to which I want to draw attention here.

Perhaps I should say a *need* for a quarrel, because this divorce of language from literature seems to be proceeding without any real awareness of its implications. To explain, I must first amplify and qualify my opening sentence, which is a generalization. The situation varies from one kind of college to another, and my description of it must be taken to apply only to the kind I have taught at, the CATs. In fact, in this matter of Liberal Studies, the CATs differ considerably from each other; any syllabus analysis of one may prove inapplicable to another; but the large problem must be essentially the same at them all, because it is shaped by the conflict between quite national forces. At the college I know, then, a considerable variety of subjects under the heading 'Liberal Studies' are taught for three or four hours a week to students for Diplomas in Technology every year of their three- or four-year course; and to students for Higher National Diplomas, somewhat less. This is not, in fact, the only non-professional work they do. Statisticians do some physics or chemistry, electrical engineers some economics, and so on. But all these qualifications do not, I think, significantly reshape my opening remark. The significant clause to add to it is that English is not one of the Liberal Studies subjects.

At my college there was a department of 'English *and* Liberal Studies', and the two subdivisions were kept quite separate on each syllabus; different people taught them; teachers usually were hired for *either* English *or* Liberal Studies. At other CATs, English is taught by a Department of Communications, or both English and Liberal Studies are taught by the Department of Industrial Administration. At others, the art of composition may be taught under the name of logic, or purely by means of criticizing the students' performances (in lecturettes and reports) in their technical specialities. What all these have in common is that composition is not taught in any connection with literature. It may be a part of logic, or of report-writing, or of management or of communications: it is not connected with reading fiction, poetry, drama. This separation, this realignment, has drastic consequences for the English teacher.

The arrangement at my college was considered to give an unusually high prestige to English; students in some years get two hours of the subject a week, which is rare elsewhere. But the effect of the separation of English from Liberal Studies was, first, that the English teacher saw each class only once a week; even if he had two hours with them, this was only one session. Second, in consequence of that first point and of other conditions of the work, he could teach only the mechanics of composition, and some semi-mechanical skills. Those conditions of the work include the educational level of the students, which makes a good deal of low-level instruction obligatory, and the attitude of the students' parent-departments (Building Science, Applied Physics, Chemical Engineering, and so on) which forbids the non-professional teacher to assign any work out of class. He is kept busy, therefore, despite the quite generous-sounding allotment of class-time, with exercises in punctuation, grammar, common errors, précis; and with the various arts of the report, the memorandum, the minute, the order, the announcement, the business letter, the journal article. He should also give those who need it some speech training, and all of them some practice in talking in public. This is very time-consuming work, and all of it must get done within that one session a week. (I should add that these are all sandwich courses; the students are in college for either four years of two terms each or for three years of three.)

Quite obviously, the English class is no place to talk about literature, even on the side. That is clear from reading the syllabus. What is less obvious – what I at least only realized after I got there – is that it is no place to talk about ideas. The English teacher cannot present his rules, his explanations, his exercises, his corrections, as part of a generally educational process – as a training in how to think. He must present them as a training in how to write reports; how to record the results of previous thinking (about chemistry or statistics) which is itself independent of his jurisdiction.

Negatively, this makes the English teacher's job less important and less satisfying than it might be; than it is in a grammar school, never mind a university. Positively, it makes the work he does have to do peculiarly difficult and dissatisfying to him. Almost anybody else, it often seems to me, could do it better than someone whose training has led him to love, say, Henry James, or D. H. Lawrence. A man who has learned to see with those eyes, to get at the truth with those techniques, above all, to love language that way, is disqualified for this job. Everything in that training has evoked a feeling for language the reverse of that required, and a feeling which he cannot merely subdue, because it *is* precisely his training; it is his intellectual personality. When he looks at a piece of language he sees certain important things, and he wants to, knows how to, share that perception with other people; but these aren't the things this subject, 'English', is concerned with. He very often does not know (in the form a teacher needs to know) the mechanics of the language; he quite rarely knows how to draw up a minute or a memorandum. More important, he finds it hard to learn and teach those things, because in some sense he dislikes them. They represent the subjugation of language, the diminishment of meaning, the defeat of his kind of truth.

This may be taken to prove a weakness in his kind of truth, a defect in his discipline, an 'aestheticism'; I so take it myself; but we must not let that comment make the fact and its consequences less important to us. The fact is that people who read English at the university with any enthusiasm today learn a love of purely literary values, as opposed to even generally humanistic, never mind generally intellectual, values. Moreover, even with the broadest training, the man who loves literature is bound to find technical English dull. Even the teacher who is not narrowly aesthetic in his approach, who loves language as the medium of thought, must think of it not as a system of symbolic logic, but as a heritage of interlocking and conflicting and many-levelled meanings already half actualized before we start to manipulate them. He wants to show how language limits, directs, confuses, suggests, people's thoughts – his students' thoughts. It is the big, confusing, necessary, everyday words that are the centre of the language for him; selflessness, truth, religion, love. Chromatography, calibrate, deoxyribonucleic acid, these are only half words to him. Language cut off from its roots in thought – multiple, metamorphic thought – is language maimed, shrunken, stuffed.

There are, in fact, only two ways of teaching English (how to write) to students of this age. Either one teaches it as a part of literature (attributing the ideal breadth to that concept) or one does not. The first way I presume most readers will be familiar with in idea, because it is followed in grammar schools. The second is most often expounded nowadays under the heading Communication. Communication is, like Liberal Studies, a new subject area, with considerable current quarrelling about its exact definition, its boundaries, and its alliances. Some of its leaders insist that language must not be, cannot be, separated from literature. Others in practice make that separation sharply, and take account of only conversational and technical uses of words. It is anyway only in books about Communication that one finds language explained and taught in dissociation from literature. Quite often such references as there are to literature betray an antipathy; more striking, in the other, the 'non-Communication' books, it is hard to find any useful advice about the non-literary uses of English It is books with titles like *Technical Communication* or *Communication in Industry* which tackle the problems facing CAT students and teachers. *The Problem of Writing* or *Effective Prose Style* will almost certainly have nothing to the point.

About the best of all these books I have found is one by R. O. Kapp, the Professor of Electrical Engineering at University College, London. It is called *The Presentation of Technical Information* and uses the term Functional English for the non-literary uses of the language; this book came out in 1948, which was early for 'Communication'. It isolates the problems of this sort of writing very precisely, and in order to do so sets up a frank, and convincing, antithesis between Functional English and Imaginative Literature;

convincing because the writer is perceptive and generous about both. Imaginative Literature, he says, uses the language of insight. It is primarily concerned with ourselves, our thoughts and feelings and reactions to experience. It discusses the outer world in terms of its meanings, either to some particular individual or to some generalized 'human' consciousness. It describes the sea to us as 'rough' and 'rude'; it does not measure the waves. This kind of English awakens self-knowledge. It rarely attempts to convey much new information. It very rarely sorts out an argument into those units and that order of units which will, in transparency of tone, in suspension of all but one order of meaning, convince the reader the most quickly, completely, usefully.

The English of imaginative literature calls on resources in the language which Functional English leaves untapped; but the reverse is also true. As Professor Kapp says, 'I doubt if a great master of English, lacking a sense of logic, could write a good elementary textbook on Physics, however well briefed he might be for the task.' One would add only that a great master of English is unlikely to have no sense of logic; but it *is* quite likely to be a manifold, laterally branching, intertwining logic, and his power to build a unitary, unidirectional stairway *may* well have atrophied. The discipline of relevance is quite different in scientific subjects, and takes form in different rules of exposition. The literary man's use of language involves understatement, overstatement, obliquity, significant juxtaposition, and so on; none of which will carry the meanings of science and technology; to say nothing of word-music, imagery, myth-making, story-telling. And Functional English is not what is left when you suppress these uses of language. If you strip those techniques from a literary discourse, you find very weak and wandering argument left behind.

English teachers tend to regard Functional English and its problems as a subdivision of creative literary composition. But this is a fallacy. One can be – one often is – highly sophisticated and even skilful in the latter while remaining clumsy and ignorant in the former. And if not clumsy, if a good expositor oneself, one may remain quite ignorant of how to teach other people the art. Professor Kapp explains at the beginning of his book how he appealed to his colleagues in English when he first realized that his graduate students needed some formal help of this kind, needed a course in exposition. He was always told either that such teaching should have been done at school or that he should go over an individual student's lab. reports with him sentence by sentence. This betrays, as he says, a complete misunderstanding of the problem. These students are not at fault in grammar or syntax so much as in logic and psychology – the logic and psychology of exposition. Exposition, he concludes, has ceased to be, or has not yet become, a part of any academic subject in England.

Since the date of his book there have been some beginnings in that direction. British, and even more American, linguists are doing work that promises a new art of exposition as part of a new approach to language as a whole. But for our purposes we need to emphasize the present drastic splitting off of English as a university and grammar-school subject (as the English teacher learns it) from English as the CAT student needs it.

A natural corollary of this is that in these textbooks of Communication, literature, and literary values, make but brief and inglorious appearances. In fact, literature is referred to often in the way best calculated to strengthen the students' prejudice against it. 'There is no point in putting literary merit into a business document,' says one, 'unless it must be done in order to get the right reaction.' Now we must not be overrefined. This is a clumsy phrasing of a sensible point; it is not (even in a book on how to write) the mark of the beast. We should not (as I suspect most English teachers of wanting to) fall on it with furious scimitars and cries of infidel dog. But if this is the way both teachers and textbooks refer to literature, even in English classes, the students' ears are going to be sealed beyond all hope against ideas they must at best find it hard to hear.

In the same book the writer explains the difference between sense, feeling, and tone, with some contrasting examples.

'In the later part of the year the leaves of the trees become brown, shrivel, and fall to the ground.' This is bare fact, sheer sense, conveying no feeling or tone.

'How strange and awful is the synthesis of life and death in the gusty winds and falling leaves of an autumnal day.' Here we find feeling as well as fact.

'Never prate to me about the beauties of autumn! It is the season of sorrow, reminding me always of my own declining days and the onset of death. As dutiful son, you should spare me such depressing thoughts.' Here we have tone, too.

Those students who have some natural taste will, of course, prefer the bare fact. Even if they know some better examples of tone and feeling, they are bound to think of literature as essentially decorative; as pretentious and false, if it asks to be taken seriously; if it describes itself as a mode of intelligence, comparable with their own physics or economics, they will scarcely understand what is meant. Those who have no natural taste will swallow these as fair representatives of literature, of art, of culture. All the students will be markedly further from any liberality of education.

And this is only a picturesque example of a weakness one finds in all these books, even in Professor Kapp's, to some degree. These books, the useful ones, are written by engineers, by lawyers, by psychologists, not by literary men, and they have the corresponding limitations. Take an old favourite still in use, R. H. Thouless's *Straight and Crooked Thinking*. This has some valuable chapters on the formal logic of arguments, but its comments on the psychology of language (never mind on specifically literary effects) invite contradiction by the naïvest student. After all, the literary man is, *ipso facto*, the supreme judge and guardian of language in half its functions. He should be ruler of the whole domain, if the split in our culture had not made that impossible for the time being. In this argument, however, we must only insist on people's recognizing these consequences of that split. Literary men seem barely capable now of even teaching their own subject – the useful, needed, demanded parts – to scientists and technologists.

The English classes at CATs are then a service, servant's work done for the benefit of other subjects, in which the students are being educated. They make no call on the English teacher's best powers, they go against his professional training. So let us suppose

that the literary man (wanting for some reason to teach students
of science) tries to join the Liberal Studies department, to become
a teacher of some other course, taking a few classes in English as
well. When *do* the students learn about ideas?

Under the heading Liberal Studies the students are taught (this
is only typical – the details vary considerably from case to case)
in the first year Current Affairs, in the second History and Philosophy of Science, in the third the Arts in Contemporary Life, and
in the fourth Communication for Management. All these headings
indicate some mixture of subjects; 'breaking down the subject-
barriers' is one of the most powerful ideas in Liberal Studies. It is
in the third year that there is some call for a discussion of literature.
But the teacher then must also, in his once-a-week sessions, give
some attention to music, painting, architecture, and so on. Such
classes always include trips to art galleries and concert halls, films
in the classroom, records, guest-lectures, discussions. Not much
work gets done. The literature is necessarily treated in much the
same way, and the English teacher cannot feel he has been
teaching his subject.

Moreover, CATs are not very big. My own had eight hundred
students, and the final expanded size envisaged by the Ministry
is about two thousand each. The Departments of Liberal Studies,
or General Studies, have only a minor, a marginal claim on the
time of those students. There is therefore a small staff, and a
teacher must be able to handle more than his own speciality.
How well qualified is the English teacher from this point of view?
One can suppose him (the sort of English teacher who might want
this job) quite able to deal with the Arts in Contemporary Life;
he may or may not be able to deal with Current Affairs; he is
most unlikely to know anything about the History and Philosophy
of Science.

These colleges are now trying to hire specialists – people with
higher degrees. They are anxious to achieve 'university status'.
(Para-universities is the official euphemism; not proto- or quasi-
but para-.) But in the case of Liberal Studies, with its mixed
subject-areas, this ambition is obviously self-defeating. Especially
in English, but importantly in all subjects these days, the man who

loves his subject will hate to teach it in dilution, or in combination, or in summary. He will think of it as a method of thought, a discipline, not as a collection of facts; much less as a gallery of curios through which everyone should be given a tour at least once in their lives. The CATs are caught between two opposite movements in modern thought; the first, from the universities, towards the purification of academic subjects; the second, from the teachers' training colleges perhaps – from the educational theorists, anyway – towards their merging. The English teacher more than anyone feels out of place, untrained for his job, in a Liberal Studies department.

There is, of course, no full-time training for the job as yet. The staff divides usually into two groups. One is made up of general-purpose teachers, most of whom taught in these colleges before they became CATs, whose talent is for getting on with reluctant classes, for benevolently correcting the uncouth, for teaching a certain amount of anything they are asked to. The other, the younger and more recently hired, are specialists in English, history or philosophy, who have also some range of interests and adventurousness of spirit. I suspect that the best teaching is still done by the first group, but the trend towards specialization is desirable as well as inevitable. It is important in a college of this kind that the Liberal Studies staff should be as highly trained, as intellectually weighty, as the other lecturers. The students are only too ready to regard their Liberal Studies hours as a relaxation from real work, as a training – one most of them *want*, of course – in useful social techniques; how to run a meeting, how to win an argument, how to discuss the events of the day, how to get on equal terms with Oxbridge students (and Oxbridge-trained managers). They are quite ready to make the distinction between education and training in favour of Liberal Studies; but what this turns out to mean is the abolition of intellectual discipline and the study of self-salesmanship. Liberal Studies must be given the dignity of serious hard work; although they must also be related to the students' extra-curricular life (its moral-intellectual aspects) more directly than, say, university courses – just because they are so much briefer. This is, after all, these students' only academic chance to meet, to realize, to understand, the other kinds of intelligence and meaning there are in the world. They won't do that by relaxed dabbling, or by learning how to make a speech.

If, then, these teachers must be specialists, but must be able to teach a number of the courses offered by the department, how well qualified is the English teacher? There are, comparatively, plenty of history teachers who will fit in very well. They have had enough training in plain exposition to be able to teach English; they know enough of Current Affairs to be able to teach that; the material of the History and Philosophy of Science is their material. But the English teacher knows very little that is useful; and he knows far too much which will hinder him.

So far everything I have said has led quite straightforwardly to one conclusion; teachers with literary training should stay out of CATs. It may have seemed unnecessary to argue so lengthily against so little opposition. But I feel a powerful opposition, a profound inner resistance, to that conclusion. It is literature these students need to be taught more than anything. Not that they are any less ignorant of the facts of history; but they are (somewhat) less ignorant of, and hostile to, its methods and meanings. Imaginative literature is, as Professor Kapp pointed out, the supreme guardian of insight, of self-knowledge, of human meanings, of things in their relation to us; it is the mode of intelligence most opposite to those the scientist and technologist himself employs. In Liberal Studies textbooks it is often pointed out that engineers need Social Studies because their jobs involve dealing with, understanding, men and women as much as iron and concrete. But it is the kind of understanding of men and women given by the study of literature which the engineer finds really remote from his own training, and just as relevant as Social Studies to the non-mechanical problems of his job.

If these students are not taught how to read, some will certainly find their way to good novels themselves; some will respond to them with feeling and understanding; but none will understand that literature, and the study of literature, is a mode of knowledge, a truth discipline, just as much as their own. If they could be taught, during their four years – and the students themselves are perfectly capable of this – to read, say, George Orwell with fairly full appreciation, and to write out their own judgements and experience in a fairly similar manner, then they would be more liberally educated than by acquiring any other new skills, equally narrowly defined.

One opposes that conclusion, that renunciation, also because there are so many teachers of English with just the missionary zeal and intellectual discipline to go into CATs and technical colleges and do the job that needs doing. Dr Leavis's students, and his students' students, believe in their work as a mode of knowledge, not just taste, as a truth discipline, and the kind of truth supremely necessary to scientists and technologists. Teachers of this quality are not easy to find. I don't know of any other subject – history, philosophy, or anything else – where you could expect to find so many intelligent and trained missionaries.

For both these reasons I would be ready, but for one thing, to argue that Liberal Studies should give up the attempt to teach a bit of everything and should concentrate on English; that for their three or four hours a week for four years (remember this in only seventy to eighty weeks of classes) the students should be taught nothing but how to read and write fairly sophisticated language. Such language would, of course, begin with Functional English, and include parts of Imaginative Literature; essays, criticism, fiction; but only reach out towards poetry and drama. Sophisticated language means sophisticated ideas, and those ideas can be non-literary, so that this education need not be as narrow as it sounds. I am thinking of books like *The Road to Wigan Pier*; in the discussion of that a great many political and sociological ideas can be examined, just as a great deal can be learned about the art of exposition. All that one does in these two directions will be useful, moreover, in the central task of recognizing, appreciating, estimating, the dramatic monologue at the heart of the book. This is no narrowly aesthetic education; it is a variety of experience and values, apprehended through the single discipline of language.

This would be the way, I suggest, to break down the subject-barriers. Liberal Studies seems to me far too desultory and dilettante in its present method – liable, in the hands of all but the best teachers, not to be an education at all. Though I would not, of course, want to supplant all the other humanities subjects with English. I would imagine students choosing either the course I describe or, for instance, a similar concentration on the History and Philosophy of Science. If they could not be offered many such alternatives within a particular college, different colleges could certainly concentrate on one or two, and the student could choose his college with that in mind.

The one thing that prevents me from arguing this case is, paradoxically, the missionary zeal of those English teachers. Would they be willing, for instance, to teach Functional English? Would they be willing, even, to teach a book like *The Road to Wigan Pier*? Could they – this is the root of the matter – come to terms with the intellectual world in which their students are being educated, the tradition they are assimilating? The teachers think *they* stand for tradition, and they mean they are the soldiers of a powerful anti-scientific faith. But the students', too, is a powerful, self-sufficient, somewhat embattled tradition. These students have the prejudice against literature (taken seriously) of all plain men in our society, plus the resentment against culture of those who have failed to get into a university (many did not get through grammar school), plus the pride of those who are trained in a rival, more masculine, more socially powerful discipline. It is no good approaching them with an offer of the Truth, with the gospel of the true religion, as if they were pagans in some more primitive culture. If you rouse their antagonism, or rather – since it is already roused – if you do not allay their antagonism, you will spend your time winning a grudging respect from the fair-minded students, not usefully teaching. The only useful way to approach them is as fellow workers in another branch of a common intellectual tradition. But how many teachers of literature could do that?

Perhaps I ought to say something here about the work I think Liberal Studies should do. My biggest conviction is that it must be taught as a subject; as a body of information ordered by its own categories, that is, which the student has to demonstrate, in class and in examination, that he has intelligently absorbed. Surely very few of us ever learn new attitudes except as a result of acquiring new information; except in subjects we already know well; and whatever may be taught in Liberal Studies, it will be new subject-matter to the students. It surely imposes a wholly unnecessary strain on the teachers to have to try to communicate the art of thinking in this or that subject, when the students know *so little about it. To run classes purely as discussion groups both disorientates the student, who in every other subject takes notes, and demands quite irrelevant performing skills from the Liberal Studies teacher. It almost inevitably produces verbal exhibitionism on both sides – debate rather than discussion – and quite inevitably makes Liberal Studies into non-work. The design of such courses should start from the realization that the students must be taught a lot of information; and that information had better not be the highly conceptual 'facts' of literature.*

That being so, the obvious subject-matter to choose is history; which has remained such a central, humanistic subject even under the stresses of the two cultures conflict, and which therefore evokes so much less obstructive antagonism. The History and Philosophy of Science (which should be presented in the first two years as history rather than philosophy) is already taught at CATs. But there are other possibilities, some of which suggest themselves when we read J. G. Crowther's 6 Great Engineers *or his* 6 Great Inventors. *There are some remarkable parallels between Edison and Mark Twain, for instance, and I can imagine a very interesting course based on comparing those two, or, more ambitiously, contrasting those two taken together with, perhaps, de Lesseps and Disraeli taken together. The method I conceive would be biographical (biography is after all the quintessential humanistic form), but would move out from the individual to, first, the society of which he was a part, and, second, his creative work.*

Edison's parallels with Twain are remarkably interesting, and between them the two men sketch out a profile of America between the Civil War and the First World War. (I will assume that the reader is familiar with Twain, and only pick on a few points in Edison's career which are either parallel or historically evocative.) Like Twain, Edison had practically no schooling, and like Twain he began his career with newspapers. At the age of twelve he was selling papers in Detroit and on the train to Port Huron, and was doing so well out of it that he could hire other boys to run stalls for him, selling papers and vegetables and fruit. During the Civil War he started printing his own paper on the train – the first time anyone had done such a thing, and he was fifteen. He persuaded a telegraph operator at Detroit to send bulletins of war news to stations along the track for him to incorporate into his paper. Later he himself became a telegrapher. As a tramp operator, he 'roughed it' for five years (like Twain's years as a travelling printer and prospector); one of his friends became a gunman in Texas, and there was a lot of shooting, gambling, and horseplay in the group.

From newspapers he moved, through telegraphy, to the stock exchange (surely the three great symbols of Gilded Age America). Almost his first invention was a stock ticker in Boston in *1868*, and he got his first big money in New York for an improvement to that. Half the incidents in his life seem to have been historically symbolic in this way. He worked for the Western Union when he first went to New York, but slept in the battery room of the Gold Indicator Company, having no money for an hotel room. At that time Jay Gould and Jim Fisk were fighting Vanderbilt on the Stock Exchange over the price of gold, which consequently shot up and down hectically; as a result, the Gold Indicator Company's transmitter broke down. Edison fixed it, and was made general manager on the spot. He immediately founded a company of electrical engineers (the first time the term was used) for the purpose of selling inventions, and almost immediately got 40,000 dollars for his improved ticker. Like Twain, he was feverishly excited by the idea of money, and loudly cynical about less materialistic attitudes to one's work, but he was, they both were, too romantic to be as worldly or as ruthless as they claimed. After he had expounded to Professor Nernst his principle that one should never work on any invention for which there is not an immediate financial return, the Professor asked him how much he'd got for his carbon filament lamp; he'd got nothing; Nernst, on the other hand, had been paid 250,000 dollars for a version of the same thing which never really worked.

Interestingly, Shaw worked in the Edison company's London offices, and derived from the American engineers he met there the image of the New Man, which he contrasted with the Eton and Oxford aristocrat in his plays. Ford worked in the Detroit Edison Power Station while he was experimenting on his automobile. Later these two high priests of American enterprise went camping together, with an entourage of journalists, to advertise the *virtues of 'roughing it'. Like Twain, Edison was a great philistine; he refused to believe his salesmen in Germany when they said the public demanded classical music in his phonograph. Like Twain, he dramatized his own primitiveness. In 1903, when he was fifty-six and had long been a millionaire, when asked the rules of his laboratory by a new employee, he spat on the floor and shouted, 'Hell! There ain't no rules around here! We are trying to accomplish somep'n.' Like Twain, he cultivated a furious temper. Like Twain, he loved publicity, and had a very flexible sense of the truth: 'We always tell the truth . . . of course, it may be deferred truth.'*

Just the recounting of this life-story, in some detail, and then Twain's, would be absorbing material for the teacher to work with. In these stories, and even more, later, in bringing out the parallels between them, he can also sketch in the political and social background of America then; the raw and feverish feeling of the times is embodied in these two lives, and all the great social forces were working on them. Moreover, the second half of both men's lives was fairly consciously lived out as social myth, and very consciously sold to the contemporary public that way. They were social history. Then some time should be spent on Edison's inventions (these students are after all technologists – their business is applied science), with emphasis on the way Edison's temperament and ideology influenced them; why he chose to work on what he did. Finally the same can be done with Twain, who was after all an entrepreneur in literature, someone who applied literary talents to new social uses and to making a fortune. The students could have been reading extracts from The Gilded Age *and* Roughing It *during the earlier part of the course.*

The treatment of this material would take at least a term, and a term and a half if the students have a three-term year. Some discussion would be possible towards the end of this period. As for de Lesseps and Disraeli, a similar treatment seems suitable, except that Disraeli would presumably be treated more as a political than as a literary figure. Their two careers, which came together so picturesquely in Disraeli's purchase of the Suez canal shares, give a profile of that Napoleonic and literary romanticism of mid-nineteenth-century Europe which contrasts with the capitalistic and proletarian romanticism of Edison's America.

There are, of course, many other patterns for a course starting from applied science. One might, for instance, contrast psychological types among the great engineers and inventors: Diesel (who committed suicide with an annotated volume of Schopenhauer in his cabin) with Parsons (the turbine inventor, an aristocratic English eccentric who read Wodehouse and Pickwick). Or one might contrast sociological types: Parsons with Westinghouse, a German New Englander of boorish and violent personality, who worked in railways and electrification; one would like to put Dreiser beside Westinghouse and Henry Adams beside Parsons. Or one might build a course on quite a different principle; one might study a particular city over twenty years, the Edinburgh of Black, Smith, Stewart, Watt, and so on, or the Birmingham of Boulton, Darwin, Watt, and Priestley. There again one could move from the application of science to industry, across general social history, to the writers of the time. Or finally one might take a decade, 1870–80, or perhaps twenty years, 1870–90, and take note both of the inventions patented then and of the writers born, seeing both as forces acting on our consciousness; one could only describe the writers, with a few extracts, but one could make connection between their alienation from their society and the transformation of that society by those inventions.

Courses of this sort seem to me to offer the best chance of liberalizing the education of technologists under the conditions now operating or foreseeable.

6. Two surveys of the literature of science

I

There is a paradox of form, a sudden reversal of argument, in this next essay, too, and it derives from a similar jaggedness of experience. Until I began to concern myself with scientific things I had found science fiction unreadable, for typical literary man's reasons. When I finally understood how to read it I was very enthusiastic for a while, and then, as quickly, disillusioned. Science fiction is, like nineteenth-century American humour, an imaginative exercise of great zest and promise, which can involve the literary reader's most excited attention, but which, quite strikingly, fails to satisfy, fails to deliver the full experience it promised. So many items in our daily news nowadays belong to that imaginative world (an enormous hole appears in a peaceful meadow; the village is cordoned off; curious crystallizations of carbon are found around the edges) that we are bound to seek out fictional treatment of such material. But its charm is more than that. Ideas and insights and perceptions, even strictly literary effects, which find no place in conventional fiction, here explode like fireworks, dazzling, but also short-lived, cut off from the central literary tradition. The split between the cultures, the purification of the literary mind, which has so specialized the subject-matter of serious fiction, has provoked a kind of rebellion, of separatist movement, which is doomed to failure, or at least to incompleteness.

Science fiction

THE statistical evidence about the readers of science fiction indicates that they are mostly scientific or technological by profession; they are also quite young, with that training not far behind them. You are told this in Kingsley Amis's *New Maps of Hell*, and it strikingly confirms your own more sensibilitarian estimate while reading. The evidence for that estimate is not so much that there is a lot to offend or bore the reader with literary training; nor even the number of allusions to scientific knowledge in the stories; it is that quite major themes of the imagination are developed there in a way that the non-scientific reader recognizes as both authentic and at the same time deeply alien to him.

Take, for instance, the theme of natural beauty. Some science-fiction writers, of course (Ray Bradbury, for example), celebrate the beauty of the earth in conventional literary style, and invent for other planets some quite sugary and fairy-tale prettiness; like Hansel and Gretel's cottage, the rocks look likely to be marzipan, and the rivers pure butterscotch. Others do extend our sensibility out beyond the ordinary; perhaps by fastening our imaginations at length on the multitude of stars out there, the galaxies of galaxies, or by conjuring up the nature we know under radically different conditions (as J. G. Ballard does in *The Drowned World*.) But the true equivalent of those beautiful lilac groves and graceful birch avenues of nineteenth-century Russian literature, those sparkling spring thaws, those nightingale summer nights, the true equivalent of those in science fiction is something like the lunar sunrise and lunar vegetation in H. G. Wells's *The First Men in the Moon*. Quotation is unfair, because both descriptions are narrative and cumulative, but these paragraphs will give a taste of what is meant to those unfamiliar with the genre.

'Look! The sunrise! The sun!'

He turned me about and pointed to the brow of the eastward cliff, looming above the haze about us, scarce lighter than the darkness of the sky. But now its line was marked by strange reddish shapes, tongues of vermilion flame that writhed and danced. I fancied it must be spirals of vapour that had caught the light and made this crest of fiery tongues against the sky, but indeed it was the solar prominences I saw, a crown of fire about the sun that is forever hidden from earthly eyes by our atmospheric veil.

And then – the sun!

Steadily, inevitably came a brilliant line, came a thin wedge of intolerable effulgence that took a circular shape, became a bow, became a blazing sceptre, and hurled a shaft of heat at us as though it was a spear.

It seemed verily to stab my eyes! I cried aloud and turned about blinded, groping for my blanket beneath the bale.

And with that incandescence came a sound, the first sound that had reached us from without since we left the earth, a hissing and rustling, the stormy trailing of the aerial garment of the advancing day. And with the coming of the sound and the light the sphere lurched, and blinded and dazzled we staggered helplessly against each other. It lurched again, and the hissing grew louder. I had shut my eyes perforce, I was making clumsy efforts to cover my head with a blanket, and this second lurch sent me helplessly off my feet. I fell against the bale, and opening my eyes had a momentary glimpse of the air just outside our glass. It was running – it was boiling – like snow into which a white-hot rod is thrust. What had been solid air had suddenly at the touch of the sun become a paste, a mud, a slushy liquefaction, that hissed and bubbled into gas.

And, in the next chapter:

One after another all down the sunlit slope, these miraculous little brown bodies burst and gaped apart, like seed-pods, like the husks of fruits; opened eager mouths that drank in the heat and light pouring in a cascade from the newly-risen sun.

Every moment more of these seed coats ruptured, and even as they did so the swelling pioneers overflowed their rent distended seed-cases and passed into the second stage of growth. With a steady assurance, a swift deliberation, these amazing seeds thrust a rootlet downward to the earth and a queer bundlelike bud into the air. In a little while the slope was dotted with minute plantlets standing at attention in the blaze of the sun.

They did not stand for long. The bundle-like buds swelled and strained and opened with a jerk, thrusting out a coronet of little sharp tips, spreading a whorl of tiny, spiky, brownish leaves, that lengthened rapidly, lengthened visibly even as we watched. The movement was slower than any animal's, swifter than any plant's I have ever seen.

In a few minutes, as it seemed, the buds of the more forward of these plants had lengthened into a stem and were putting forth a second whorl of leaves, and the slope that had seemed so recently a lifeless stretch of litter was now dark with the stunted olive-green herbage of bristling spikes that swayed with the vigour of their growing.

This is very unlike, say, Turgenev's or Tolstoy's descriptions, but it deserves comparison with them. This is writing inspired by a radically different, but equally vivid, response of the imagination to nature. Like Turgenev's, Wells's description is beautifully exact observation, suffused with the excitement of its human meanings. But Turgenev looks back on an achieved, a perfect reality. Wells leaps forward to what could be elsewhere, might have been, may yet be.

Or take the theme of society and the individual. There is a lot of interesting work on this in science fiction, and a lot of the best is by Frederick Pohl and C. M. Kornbluth. They are essentially witty writers, and most of their work is in some relation to satire; whether its form is the short story ('The Midas Touch') the extended parable (*The Space Merchants*) or the darker-coloured, more daring *Wolfbane*. Perhaps the characteristic difference between their work and conventional fiction's treatment of the same material can be brought out by contrasting their *Search the Sky* with Evelyn Waugh's *Black Mischief*. Both present, to comic effect, a series of contrasting social groups, linked by an adventurous plot which is also partly the agent of the book's satirical meanings. But in *Search the Sky* we visit a whole planet ruled by the old, one ruled by women, one ruled by the stupid, and so on; with a large-scale invention of the laws, customs, political and industrial organization, which derives from that cardinal fact. The humour of the book, its entire interest, is in political systems and their specimens; not in persons and their distortion by a system, as in the conventional fiction.

'Conventional' fiction, of course, includes a hundred varieties. I choose one or two in each case to characterize it. This seems to me justified, if one admits the mere possibility of contrasting it with another form. Fiction has so encroached on other literary forms over the last hundred years that it includes some examples of almost every literary possibility. We must distinguish some as more properly or essentially fictional than others. There are, of course, many qualifications one ought to make to my generalizations; but the mere possibility of making such comparisons seems to me important enough, and ignored enough, to deserve dramatization.

When conventional fiction takes history as a major theme it treats it, typically, after the manner of *Buddenbrooks* or *War and Peace*. It describes, that is, the fortunes of two or three generations of one family, and through them the commercial, artistic, political trends of the times; or at most, like Tolstoy, it describes representative figures in a great national struggle, so that we have a turning-point in European history realized for us. Even in these two examples, the literary form bulges and groans under the strain of so much content, so much history. But in Walter M. Miller's *A Canticle for Leibowitz* we go through a complete cycle of human history, from earliest desert-life beginnings to the rediscovery and self-destructive re-use of nuclear power. The historical imagination is encouraged to a much freer play; the writer invents a new version of the Renaissance, re-creates with variations the life of a medieval monastery. There are some beautiful moments in the book, some imaginative feats that succeed by the most conventional standards, but the thing to emphasize here is the oddity, for the literary man, and yet the authenticity, of its treatment of a familiar theme.

We also find in this book a typical science fiction way of handling the religious theme. This is the way followed in James Blish's *A Case of Conscience*, too; the other important method of serving our moral-religious sensibility – to invent a humanoid race lacking some important component of our nature, aggressiveness, sexuality, scepticism, and to explore the cultural differences this would bring – that method seems not to have attracted such intense imagination. Blish and Miller both take over the whole elaborate structure of the Roman Catholic church, dogmatic, liturgical, disciplinary, with some bold fictional variations, and invent new moral and theological problems for it to solve. A striking feature of both books is their sympathy with the Church they describe. The enormous excitement of the idea of God and his incarnation and a divinely guided church are here presented just as vividly, and just as seriously, as in Graham Greene or François Mauriac; and yet they are quite incommensurably different. Instead of probing into rationalistic experience to expose its limitedness, its incoherence, its inadequacy, under strain; or introducing unnatural or supernatural phenomena in close combination with the most ruthless naturalism; instead of this the science-fiction writer moves outward, constructs new religious systems, applies them to new worlds.

Both literatures now have a sense of the precariousness of human civilization, and of the inwardness of the threat that hangs over it. That sense in science fiction is, of course, rendered much more by forecasts of future cataclysms and pictures of other societies than it is in conventional fiction; this much was implied in the differences already discussed. But it is worth noticing also the part played in creating this mood by devices like that in H. G. Wells's 'The Sea-Raiders'; in which a man-eating kind of octopus appears off the coast of Devon, kills a few people, and disappears. In its unambitious way, this story also stirs the imagination with a sense of the unexplored possibilities of nature, the untamed dangerousness of life. But it involves no projection into the future or into another natural order. Its procedure is simply first to evoke, and then to disturb, the prosperous social complacency of Edwardian England. Now this much might be said of many ordinary novels about that period. What then makes this science fiction? Partly the octopuses themselves (asking the reader to fear them), but also the author's concentration on social machinery in his evocation of that society, and his frank use of characterological cliché to the same effect.

Lastly, even individual psychology can be explored in science fiction, though with effects very different from those achieved in ordinary literature. J. G. Ballard, for instance, claims that 'inner space' as much as outer can be the science-fiction writer's field. In his novel, *The Drowned World*, the hero undergoes in his own psyche the regression of the whole species, the whole planet, towards a less formed, less conscious, inchoate state. His unconscious gradually subdues and submerges his conscious mind, just as the ocean drowns London, and that ocean-unconscious is warmer, drowsier, more animal, more turbulent, altogether more female-potent, than the one we know. Even here, in presenting purely introspective material, it is the manipulation of external reality, the element of large-scale literal change, which marks the science-fiction treatment. The internal drama is no more extreme than conventional fiction in modern times has often presented; for instance, Gerald Crich's state of mind just before his death in *Women in Love*; indeed, Lawrence being a great writer, the extraordinariness there is in the profounder sense more extreme. It is the transformation of nature which is science-fictional; and it is this also which is responsible for the book's considerable successes. *The Drowned World* has been described as *The Heart of the Matter* told from Kurtz's point of view. But in order to give Kurtz's point of view, a writer would *have* to (that is, he would gain immensely if he did) make the science-fictional changes to the story; make the external world, the world of Brussels and the Congo Company, undergo transformations as dramatic as his feelings about them do in Conrad's story.

These particular differences of treatment derive from, express, serve, a general difference of sensibility in the readers and writers. This is why we recognize Kingsley Amis's statistics as confirming our impression; these stories are written for scientists. The scientific sensibility is oriented towards the species, the literary towards the individual. This is not to say that the scientific mind is not interested in individuals. That would be just as much a libel as to say that literary people are not interested in the fate of the race. But the scientific mind is comparatively uninterested, absolutely not-very-interested, in the multitudinous ways in which human individuals differ from each other, the multitudinous details of manner and creed and interest by choice of which, conscious or unconscious, they make up personalities for themselves, and achieve – to the degree they do – the great personal qualities of power, generosity, intelligence, love, and so on. The scientific mind is interested in individuals not as persons but as specimens, exemplifying laws of cause and effect; genetic, medical, sociological laws. From another point of view, its characteristic movement is outward, away from those rich confused insights in which knowing and feeling and fundamental revaluation are all acting on each other, towards a harder clearer activity on problems so defined as to be resolvable. It is extroverted; it may look inside a human being, but it treats what it finds there as objective reality; it does not combine with its recognition of the facts a search for the right emotional response to them, to the act of recognition itself, to the act of search. It is passionately interested in the external world of Nature and human artifice; the literary

mind is likely to be desultory and dilettante about them, passionate
about self-knowledge and self-achievement and those social structures which serve them. The scientific mind is interested in the
large features of whole societies; the literary mind is interested in
particular friendships and small group relationships.

It is because of this fundamental orientation of the scientific
mind that science fiction, serving readers with scientific training,
treats imaginative themes in the ways it does; that it invents new
forms of nature, new societies, huge sweeps of space and time, that
it moves outward and onward and generalizes, that it concentrates
on social machinery and employs characterological cliché. All of
which are ways a literary man would not choose; more than that,
taken all together, he *could* not choose them, because they add up
to a radically opposed sensibility. You can see the importance of
this conflict when you reflect on H. G. Wells's fiction. Wells was
passionately interested in the species as a whole; he was not passionately interested in, though he was inquisitive and perceptive
about, persons. And it is just this which spoils his ordinary novels.
An interest in individuals is not, of course, to be measured by a
writer's production of vivid characters, in any Dickensian sense.
In a low-powered way, Wells was quite good at that; quite as
good as, say, Henry James. But James was a much finer novelist;
because he was always exploring the possibilities of personal
quality.

The relationship of science fiction to the scientific sensibility is
demonstrated over again in any reading of, say, *The Scientific
American*. In nearly any issue, half the articles will suggest to you
some idea of the kind of which these novels are based. This occurs
not only in articles about future technological developments; or
about psychological studies of the brain mechanism; it occurs
even more in studies of animal behaviour. Take the trophallaxis
of the army ants, for instance; these ants keep kissing and caressing
each other, licking and nuzzling, and as they do so they trade
certain glandular secretions; each takes what is necessary to him,
and gives what is necessary to the other. Keep the larvae separate
from the workers, or the workers from the queen, and they die.
This kissing and embracing also regulates the whole army's

rhythm of life: its alternation of fixed bivouac and nomadic wandering; because when the worker ant clutches a cocooned pupa, if the latter is still sleeping, the worker is calmed and soothed, but if it is quickening and twitching, the worker is excited – other workers snatch it from him and from each other – and the general excitement leads to the army's striking camp. It is as a result of this handling, also, that the pupa is released from its cocoon.

I take these details from an article by T. C. Schneirla and Gerard Piel. In a few pages they sketch there a whole society picturesquely like and unlike our own, and with its own characteristic triumphs and disasters. These are the ants which march in columns of a hundred thousand each, and plunder everything in their path; and which can, under certain circumstances, form themselves into an endless circular column, and literally march themselves to death.

It is surely undeniable that our imaginations, our profoundest imaginations, are powerfully stimulated by images of this kind; and that it is in science fiction, not in conventional novels, that such stimuli are the starting-points for major imaginative efforts; that in other words there is a scientific sensibility even in matters of the arts. This seems to me a powerful argument against those who claim that there is no second culture. There is certainly a second sensibility, which is always *tending* (it is in a minority position in the world of publishers and producers) to create hobbies, habits, entertainment, and even art, for itself. This activity is, of course, much stimulated by the split between the two cultures, which makes so much of conventional culture anti-scientific. Science fiction is only the most picturesque example of this activity.

Science fiction has received little serious critical attention, and has been left largely in the hands of a few men in each country. These men have decided which writers shall appear in print, which shall be publicly praised, what good science fiction is, what science fiction is. They are most typically, in America, the editors of the science-fiction magazines, and in England – since the magazines are mostly American – the compilers of anthologies.

It is in the anthologies that science fiction reaches the general reader, and this is, of course, a small fraction of that published. Moreover, it is when a writer has had a story in an anthology, or when he has had a mention by a reviewer (often an anthologist himself on other days of the week) that he may persuade someone to publish his novel.

In England the best known of these men are Kingsley Amis, Robert Conquest, Brian Aldiss, and Edmund Crispin. They all take a very similar attitude to the genre, and follow a very similar taste; the same writers, praised for the same virtues, appear in all their collections. This taste is convincing (certainly one would rather trust it than plunge into those murky magazines for neglected pearls), but their comments on the theory of the genre sometimes puzzle and dissatisfy.

The most important case is their theory of science-fiction characterization. It is universally agreed that the people one meets in these stories, even the good ones, are unconvincing and uninteresting by comparison with quite a low grade of conventional fiction; they are neither freshly observed, deeply explored, nor carefully selected; they are often pulp magazine puppets, and badly manipulated at that. Everyone is agreed about this fact; but people differ widely about its interpretation. For most readers with literary training, this disposes of science fiction altogether, because, unconsciously or not, they identify literature with the moral-psychological exploration of personal relations. The anthologists, of course, insist that this fiction cannot be judged by that criterion, because it is attempting something quite different. So far one must agree with them; but they go on to maintain that science fiction *cannot* offer interesting characterization, because that would over-involve the reader in the individual character, and distract his attention from the species or the society or the experiment which is the main subject. This argument I find unconvincing. The kind of characterization Lawrence devised for *Women in Love* allows the writer to focus our attention on states of mind which are common to all the major characters and which must be quite impersonally understood as crisis conditions for modern human consciousness. And if conventional characterization is dissolved away there, naturalistic plausibility, that other novelist's sanctity so unattainable for science fiction, is equally jettisoned. And yet the psychology of the action is of the richest interest. Lawrence in some sense cancels the characters out as individuals; as he said, he was interested in the element, the carbon, not the individual diamond; and this could surely be the manifesto of the science-fiction writer. Perhaps a simpler case is Kafka: his characters are not allowed to absorb one flicker of our attention more than the writer wants for his large allegorical purposes. Science-fiction writers waste a good deal more detail and feeling on their characters than either Lawrence or Kafka. It is true, of course, that the latter's characters are not sociological specimens of the kind that serve science fiction's purposes best; but they are specimens, and so do demonstrate that a generalization in character can be expressed without clichés of literary effect. It is true also that if the science-fiction writer creates characters of comparable interest he will be transcending the *limits* of the scientific sensibility as defined above. The anthologists imply that in that case he would cease to be a science-fiction writer. But it is a peculiar kind of advocacy that identifies a genre with its limitations. We would not dream of doing that with conventional fiction. But the defenders of science fiction obviously do not expect from their genre the inventiveness and self-transcendence first-class writing always manages.

They seem similarly timid in other of their comments. They often insist, for instance, that what we should go to science fiction for is 'tales of wonder'; which reduces the genre to intellectual childishness. Tales of wonder I can do without; and anyway a book like *A Canticle for Leibowitz* is not to be summed up by such a phrase. Again, Edmund Crispin, in his introduction to *Science Fiction 3*, describes the whole genre as 'anti-humanist'; it represents the triumph of the environment over the individual as a subject for fiction, and exults in demonstrating the limitations of man. This is surely an unnecessary surrender to the people whose contempt he is combating. Those critics who identify the humanities with literature, and humanism with a literary sensibility to personal relations, necessarily find no true humanism in either science or science fiction. But, in fact, what one goes to these books for is a manifestation of humanism one cannot find in conventional literature; not in the sense of an exaltation of humanity, but in the sense of a full engagement of different human powers, harmoniously co-operating to examine some range of human experience. Science fiction examines an individual's environment, our environment, with an inventiveness of imagination usually reserved for his personal relationships; and we are, after all, interested in both.

Finally, one is puzzled that the anthologists don't demand more from their genre. The quality of the scientific explanation in a story, for instance, counts for quite a lot. It is not merely that to fall below a given low standard disqualifies; for Fred Hoyle's *The Black Cloud* survives some quite inept novelistic technique because of real conviction in its explanations. Again, one is often prompted to ask whether the short-story form is not a severe disadvantage to science fiction. There is such a quantity of information to be conveyed to the reader, such a transformation of half his presuppositions, before he can begin to respond rightly to the dialogue or the gestures in front of him. He cannot grasp the significance of the most harmless-looking exchange if he does not know that on this planet men have two heads each; and scratching one of them is a sexual invitation of the grossest kind; and so on. One must admit that many science-fiction writers (Pohl and Kornbluth are striking examples) have become very adept at compressing and conveying all this with no separate paragraphs. But they are thereby limited to one or two obvious points, and kinds of point; their tone is thin; they can't ask you to believe very fully in all this, because they haven't time to make it fully real to you. Edmund Crispin complains of the wastefulness of the genre. Surely it is the short-story form which causes this. *A Canticle for Leibowitz* was a short story first, and became a full-length novel only after several year's more work. One would like to see this happen to nearly all the best science-fiction stories, and one wonders why the anthologists do not suggest it.

All these oddities of particular treatment are reflected in a general uncertainty of tone, a general uneasiness about the status of their genre. Or perhaps it is not uncertainty but intractability. They are consistent enough in the way they talk about it, and that way is characterizable enough, but it is eccentric, tortuous, and full of exclusions, full of dismissals of those who take another tone, any other tone, those who don't take science fiction seriously, or who take it too seriously. One is forbidden to treat it in the way one treats any other kind of literature, anything else at all. This is symbolized in their use of 'sf'; an aggressive unhighbrowness, a truculent appropriation of other people's language. In *New Maps of Hell* Kingsley Amis dodges and swerves his way through his readers, hugging the ball to himself and drawing near this or that other writer only to fend him off with a punch in the face ('trend-hound' or 'pundit'). What does this combination of timidity and aggressiveness mean?

The source of the uneasiness is evident as soon as one concentrates on their problem. How much *can* one claim for science fiction's achievement? One is startled by the disparity between that and its promise. Though the best of these novels excite the imagination in dozens of ways, they never really satisfy it. Whenever one draws contrasts between them and the best of conventional fiction (like those in the first part of this essay) one becomes very uneasy. They are too disparate. And it will not do to say that they are dissimilar; both are doing the same kind of thing, treating the same themes, following the same morality, exciting the same emotions. But those emotions are never as full when we read science fiction. Contrast between the two kinds of writing is justified, but comparison, qualitative comparison, is impossible. Science fiction is finally literature, and must be judged by literary standards; and by those standards it is both remarkably interesting (even impressive) and unarguably unsatisfying – thin, flat, mono-dimensional. Why?

It will not do to say that this is still a young genre, insufficiently prestigious, and that when first-class talent begins to work in it, then we shall get first-class fiction. The trouble is that some of the talent is quite remarkable, if one admits *any* significant difference between talent and achievement; it is the nature of the performance that limits our response. It is true that most of these writers have quite simple things to learn about writing which any 'literary' novelist could teach them. But if you tidy up the prose and sharpen up the dialogue on a few pages of their stories, you will see that it does not make any important difference to your response. Nor is it a matter merely of introducing the serious concerns of conventional fiction. There are pieces in which the two kinds of material lie side by side, merely harming each other. There is an opposition between them. And even in *A Canticle for Leibowitz* or *The Drowned World* there is a curious crystallization of pure promise, pure possibility; one recognizes a striking idea, and watches it quite strikingly carried through, but the satisfaction it brings is not commensurate.

The key surely is in that word opposition. The anthologists say that the genre exists in a state of potentiality. But is it not rather a state of contradictions? Science fiction is not a genre, I would suggest, but a sub-genre; by which I mean a kind of writing which cannot develop into forms which engage major talents and deliver major meanings, though it can reinvigorate the forms of conventional literature by merging into them. The classic example of a sub-genre I know is American humour in the last century.

By American humour I mean that body of comic writing, mostly first-person, anecdotal, and dialect, which was published in American newspapers and magazines after 1820, and was in full flood by 1850–60. Its characteristic forms included the tall tale, the dialect monologue, the adventures of some stock character, encounters with some mythical animal (the white horse of the plains, the Big Bear of Arkansas, Moby Dick), stories of riverboat gamblers and frontier scouts. The sensibility of this writing was just as opposed to that of conventional contemporary literature as is science fiction's today; in a quite different way. It expressed the uneducated, unpolished, unprivileged proletariat, defiantly asserting itself far from the centres of propriety and education. At the same time it produced work of great literary interest. Its language is full of the boldest imagery, swinging between hyperbole and burlesque in a world of its own where the two are not antithetical. Its stock characters are genuinely fabulous. And though its effects are largely comic, it expresses also a savage cynicism, a profound melancholy, a preoccupation with death and violence, an irrepressible vitality and an arrogant self-assertion.

The conventional American literature of the time looked pale beside this. Caught between the sophisticated traditionalism of Europe, and this antinomian vitality, it had nothing but a genteel moralism to call its own. This was one of the dilemmas that drove Henry James out of his native land. To an observer of the Fifties it might have seemed (to many it did) that young American writers must learn to work in this American mode; and that when first-class talents were applied to it, first-class fiction would result. The interesting thing is that this did not happen.

Melville achieved something of the kind in *Moby Dick*; but this was something no subsequent writer could follow up: a literary *tour de force*, comparable with *Ulysses*. It was Twain and Whitman who raised this material to the dignity of regular literary genres: Whitman by the largeness of his vision and his massive persistence, Twain by his brilliant talents and his enormous popularity. In the work of both the new material quarrelled fatally with the forms into which it was now cast. (This is a controversial opinion, which it would need some length of argument to substantiate. I can only say here that I have argued the case in *Re-appraisals*.) What surely needs no proving is that American literature has not, in fact, apprenticed itself to them; any more than to, say, Henry James and T. S. Eliot, whose way of handling their American heritage was so non-'American'. Twain's kind of humour is now found mainly in comic strips and Disney cartoons. The 'American' material has returned again to the world of entertainment.

This happened, surely, because of the conscious opposition between its sensibility and that of literature proper. It expressed an anti-literary sensibility, and therefore could not (except in incidental, eccentric, ancillary ways) serve those young writers who wanted to create a great new literature. For the same reason I foresee the same fate for science fiction. Whether in some other society the major literary forms could be at the service of the sensibility of science fiction, we can only guess. But amongst us there is room for only one set of major forms, and one scheme of sensibility, at a time; and whatever sets itself in opposition to that must be starved not only of readers and writers but even of full achievement. Science fiction is anti-literary (opposed to the sensibility of *our* literature) in its treatment of characters, of nature, of history, of society, and so on; its writers have undertaken major imaginative enterprises without attempting minor literary standards of style and characterization. That is why its commentators identify it with its limitations (with the literary things it does *not* do) and why they are so uneasy in their tone about it. For this reason, though it has developed certain literary virtues very strikingly, I predict that it will remain unsatisfying. Writers will appear who will be able to make use of its subjects and treatments, in combination with orthodox literature's exploration of personalities; but their work will not be science fiction, because those elements will be minor, will be incidental and ancillary.

It will, however, be vivid with the infusion of that new life which science fiction brings, just as, for instance, Hemingway and Fitzgerald owed some of their vividness and freshness to Twain and Whitman's work. For, genre or sub-genre, this fiction brings with it an atmosphere of literary possibility which a writer can find hardly anywhere else today. When he puts down one of these short stories or novels, he finds his imagination reverberating with a dozen possibilities of rewriting it, and of related subjects. It is a minor reason for trying to end the split between the two cultures that if literary people knew enough science – that is, shared the scientific sensibility to some extent – they would be able to make this reinvigorating transfusion.

When I re-read that essay I am conscious how sceptical many literary readers will be, just because they assume that any act of the imagination, however scientific its object, must be non-scientific in character; that, in other words, science fiction is simply a kind of fiction and has no intrinsic connection with science. They grant, of course, some leap of the intellect in the construction of a scientific hypothesis, but they deny, implicitly, that this scientific imagination can have the function (by which, surely, we define imagination) of connecting different categories of our experience, and particularly of connecting the remoter ones to those nearer the faculties of choice, of value, of love.

There is a pervasive assumption that 'science' (scientific knowledge and scientific training) can have no close or fruitful connection with 'life' (the processes of sympathizing with, understanding, judging people, let's say) of the kind the humanities have. One of the most formidable formulations of this prejudice is Dr Johnson's remark to the effect that we are always moralists, but only sometimes mathematicians. The assumption is always made (when that formula is quoted in this context, at least) that the humanities and moralizing are very closely connected; so they are, though they are also distinct; but the assumption is also made that science has no such connections with moralizing.

Another, more modern version is this passage from T. S. Eliot's Notes Towards the Definition of Culture.

It tends, of course, to form minds which will be set to think only in terms of impersonal and inhuman forces, and thereby to de-humanize the students. Being occupied with humanity only in the mass, it tends to separate itself from ethics; being occupied only with that recent period of history during which humanity can most easily be shown to have been ruled by impersonal forces, it reduces the proper study of mankind to the last two or three hundred years.

This is said of academic training in the social sciences, but the objection is to the scientific method as such.

One can reply to Dr Johnson that mathematics serves our central moral preoccupations as much as grammar; and to T. S. Eliot that the tendency to 'de-humanize' the students is only one among many, and a feeble one. But the only effective response must be the demonstration of how such studies can, in fact, 'humanize'. The last essay tried to show how they can arouse sensibility in the literary genre of fiction. For another example, consider these three sentences.

The variability was in part occasioned by the usual night noises. When a lamb bleated or a windmill creaked, the neurotic sheep's sensitive heart immediately accelerated. No such changes in heart rate could be detected in the normal sheep.

Surely no one would deny that a passage like that sets working the poem-making faculties in all of us; and that it does so with the author's implicit consent. Let me set those lines in their context. (It comes from 'Conditioning and the Emotions', by H. S. Liddell.)

All of our neurotic sheep and goats exhibited undue sensitivity to any situations which seemed to imply danger. Even the most feeble and innocuous change in the environment, if sudden, elicited an exaggerated alarm reaction and preparation for flight. For several nights we counted the heart rates of the normal and neurotic sheep without disturbing them as they rested in the barn. From the chest piece of a stethoscope strapped to the animal a long, thick-walled rubber tube conducted the heart sounds to the listening observer in a small shed outside the barn. A normal sheep's heart beat slowly and steadily throughout the night. By contrast a neurotic animal's heart rate was rapid and highly variable, with frequent irregularities (premature beats). The variability was in part occasioned by the usual night noises. When a lamb bleated or a windmill creaked, the neurotic sheep's sensitive heart immediately accelerated. No such changes in heart rate could be detected in the normal sheep.

This comes from the article from which I also quoted the sentence about solving the 'problem of emotion' (p. 98). I think a literary man would have assumed in the author of that sentence a philistinism, an incapacity for flexible and aesthetic modes of apprehension, a lack of that imagination I defined before. But anyone who is sensitive to language will recognize here an energetic, spontaneous but controlled, interplay of multiple meanings; which is incidentally also one of the characteristic modes of modern literature. It is, for instance, the mode in which Nabokov works, and this passage, with slight alterations, could be made indistinguishable from chapters of his. The reader's mind moves to and fro between the simplest meaning and its subtler suggestions, the external observation and its internal applications, with the intellectual gaiety of parts of Lolita. *This is exactly what we mean by imagination; it is even strikingly like acts of the literary imagination; and yet it is strictly scientific. It is not a literary man writing about science.*

And it is not only in such 'literary' ways that scientific knowledge and scientific training lead one to leaps of the imagination, interconnection of the categories. Religious sensibility also can be fostered by science. Much scientific work leads the mind up and out to those enormous distances of size before which reason quails; or to those recurrent glimpses of being itself; to half the sources of all religious feeling. Moreover, it leads one out of those complexities of self-interrogation, those orgies of metaphor-making, in which so much potential religious feeling gets dissipated amongst literary people. In Corti's book on Teilhard de Chardin, Father Jarrett-Kerr puts it that there are two opposite approaches to religion, that of the

Scale of Nature theologians, like Gore, Temple, and de Chardin, and, at the other extreme, that of Marcel and the Existentialists. The latter is characteristically literary, with all the weaknesses as well as the strengths that brings. De Chardin himself, with his Christian Hegelianism, his serene humanism, is clearly the scientist as theologian; it is unfortunate that his attempt to adapt nineteenth-century progressivism and traditional Christianity to each other seems almost unique today, and is instinctively distrusted. The average cultured mind finds the idea of progress crude.

De Chardin's historical progressivism reminds us also of how the literary man is almost condemned to a cyclic view of history, or at least a cyclic feeling for history. It is hard for him to regard anyone later as an advance on Shakespeare, or even on Homer, in literary technique or in general understanding. Whereas Descartes' mathematics was (in the most important sense) an advance on Archimedes'; indeed, all of us know more mathematics, have more mathematical skill, than Archimedes. These are paradigms of two profoundly different schemes of history of all kinds, intellectual, moral, and social. As compulsive patterns of interpretation, of intellectual temperament, both are equally limited. We have heard enough about the crudity of the idea of progress; the idea of the continual cycle is crude, too, as it is usually applied. And to anyone at the mercy of either scheme, what a relief and release to see the explanatory power, the truthfulness, of the other.

Poetry, religion, history, the scientific imagination has a great deal to offer all of them, and its interaction with them could constitute a culture, an education, a humanization, to use T. S. Eliot's term. It is only the scientist's presentation of science — especially in scientific training —which makes this proposition questionable. Teachers of science don't make a point of demonstrating their subject's interactions with other modes of intelligence, as teachers of literature do. I have more to say about that in my next essay.

II

This last essay is my attempt to write something useful rather than speculative or controversial. It tries to sum up the results of my reading for four years in ways that might help other people following a similar path. I was about to resume my normal career, in which necessarily even my outside reading is most dictated by what I am teaching, and this was the legacy of the interlude, the roomful of books to sort out and give away. It is not, of course, comprehensive; no more than the previous essay does it attempt to include references to all the books worth reading in the area.

Science non-fiction

The convulsed, contorted humanist, impaled on the accusation of the two cultures, will come at last (if he is a man of good will) to the defence, 'But what can one *do* about it? What can *I* do about the fact that I am so shamefully ignorant of everything scientific? You don't expect me to start back with fifteen-year-old physics, and to put in – where? with whom? – a five years' apprenticeship to another trade which would be the best five I could give my own? And if I don't do that, I might as well do nothing. Without it, I can't read the adult books, and the baby books, the popularizations, can't give me that experience of a different intellectual discipline you say I need. Science is too hard, too professional, too pure; too hard for dilettantism, too professional for amateurs, too pure for any meditative, imaginative participation. I can't move into and out of it as I can other fields of knowledge; I can't *combine* the little science I do know with my literature and my history. And that's why I said – you see, I was right after all – that's why I said it is not one of the humanities, not a part of culture.'

I think this argument is largely justified, as far as it concerns the opportunities actually available to humanists to educate themselves in science. And if it were wholly justified, of course, the accusation of the two cultures would be blunted; it would describe merely the sort of situation about which nothing can be done – at least, not by the individual. But the assumption there that this professionalism and this purity derive from the *nature* of science is false. They derive only from a mistaken understanding of science; one which has, admittedly, dictated the way science is taught, the way it is talked about, the way it is presented to scientist and non-scientist alike, the way most of its esoteric and exoteric books are written. But the reader can discern, putting together the very best of those books, some outline of a quite different understanding of science, and consequently of a literature of science which would be available to the humanist in a quite different degree, and consequently of a way in which – so far as the individual is concerned – the two cultures wound could be healed.

In fact, one does not have to piece together that other understanding for oneself. In the series of books called *The Ancestry of Science*, by Stephen Toulmin and June Goodfield (and in other of Dr Toulmin's books), it is worked out for us in full philosophical and historical detail. Science is presented as a series of ideas about nature, and questions testing those ideas; questions which are, of course, implemented by a severely disciplined method of reasoning and experimenting. But the apparatus and the calculations we tend to identify with science, even the experiments and the scientific method, are subordinate to those ideas about nature. Moreover, those ideas occur in forms which remain substantially the same throughout history. Famous alternatives we find in the Greeks, like the rivalry between atoms-in-the-void and some sort of continuum as the ultimate theory of matter, still recur today, and the choice of either one or the other carries immense consequences for the scientist's whole work. And, to quote from a recent essay by Dr Toulmin (in *The History and Philosophy of Science Newsletter 2*),

The questions about the scale and layout of the world-stage, which preoccupied Anaximander in the sixth century BC, are still being argued between Fred Hoyle and Martin Ryle today. The basic Athenian puzzles about the fundamental *dramatis personae* of Nature are argued today by men like Werner Heisenberg and David Bohm. And problems about the time-scale and plot of the drama through which Nature unfolds, which were raised by Empedocles five hundred years before Christ, are at issue again today when Urey and Oparin, Pirie and Bernal debate the origin of life on earth.

Problems and questions of this kind are, of course, essentially similar to those which concern philosophy, and indeed poetry, and all the humanities. There is a range of such questions, *all* of which concern every thinking man, but some of which particularly attract some people; scientists are those people who are particularly attracted by the scientific questions. All these questions are investigated in the same general way, which constitutes the Western intellectual tradition; but each group of questions has its own methods, which constitute a particular discipline.

This is not to deny the progressive character of scientific knowledge, which differentiates it from the arts, but to stress its cyclic character, which it shares with them. It stresses also the contribution to science of non-'Scientists' (meaning by Scientists those white-coated priests of the pointer-reading we allow to frighten us from our interest in nature); the essential contributions made by craftsmen, philosophers, priests, amateurs, mystics, alchemists, and so on. Above all, it stresses the directing role of the intellectual imagination. A scientist's questions are determined by the range of possible answers he foresees, that range is determined by his presuppositions and his interests, those presuppositions and even more those interests are determined by the general scientific *consciousness* of his day. Following up this idea, it is easy to trace the influence of general ideas – by no means purely scientific in their origin, never mind in their application – on actual work in the laboratory. The great chain of being inspired a good deal of research in eighteenth-century biology, Mendeleyev's table of elements in nineteenth-century chemistry, and Bode's Law for a hundred years in astronomy. To give just one example in more detail (taken from Feather's biography of Rutherford) it took fifty years for Faraday's results with electrolysis to be interpreted as indicating the existence of a *unit* of electricity. Those results now seem to us to *demand* that interpretation; indeed, if the phrase has any meaning, they do demand it; and this was a period of great scientific activity, conducted under the banner of objective speculation and logical economy. Nevertheless, for fifty years this particular logical simplification was not achieved; just because the image of an electric fluid, and the mathematical machinery for interpreting the readings to suit that image, so dominated the imagination of scientists then – even Maxwell's. They *saw* the fluid; it was presupposed in a hundred other explanations; to eliminate it would deprive them of something they were used to and relied on.

From this point of view, then, science is an exercise of the whole mind, including the imagination, just as history and literature are – it is, in fact, one of the humanities. And once you have assimilated this idea you find it amply illustrated in the work of other scholars in the history and philosophy of science: in Koyré's *From the Closed World to the Infinite Universe*, Gillispie's *The Edge of Objectivity*, and Hall's *From Galileo to Newton*, to name but three.

But the history and philosophy of science is an academic subject, which demands systematic study. Moreover, it does not offer to teach the reader any science. The humanist who finds himself simply and disablingly ignorant will need to read another kind of book as well. He will need to read science-for-the-layman. It is with books of this humble class that the present essay is mostly concerned, and the theory of science expounded above is there only because it confirms and explains and guides our taste in them. Because it helps us make an adult activity out of reading what our humanist called 'baby books'.

It confirms our tentative belief that in science are things of interest to us, things of the same nature as the subject-matter we ourselves deal in. It explains where one centre of their interest lies; in those general ideas, those configurations of the scientific imagination, which direct the scientist's efforts in this rather than that direction, make this rather than that feature of a reaction interesting to him. And it guides us to, for instance, reject 90 per cent of these books as mere (and bad) popularization. Not that we should despise popularization as such (I have argued elsewhere what a foolish snobbery that is), but we are bound to demand something more when we are studying science, just because it is our most serious imagination which brings us to it and is involved with it. That something more I would like to call 'humanization'; deriving the word from 'humanism' and 'the humanities', and excluding the connotations that 'human', 'humane', 'humanity' must evoke. I mean that I expect the writer of science-for-the-layman to find those aspects of his special subject which both I and a scientist can take with equal seriousness and equal comprehension; he will include explanations for my benefit which the scientist will not need, but of the kind which he can enjoy; and he will relate them to non-scientific issues which are also presented with a sophistication that satisfies an educated man. This formula leaves a lot of room for variety, because there are a hundred tones and methods of discourse which satisfy an educated man, one for each of his hundred moods. But there are two hundred which do not satisfy him. And all of those are prominent in the contemporary literature of science-for-the-layman.

It is unsatisfying, for instance, to have loud jokes made throughout a difficult piece of exposition. It is unsatisfying to have references to juke-boxes and the twist offered us as a consolation for our uneasiness with a subject like photosynthesis. It is unsatisfying to have commonplaces of history (the Armada, let's say) described to us in picture language. It is unsatisfying to have some scientist's problem compared for our benefit to his cat's efforts to get some fish out of a covered dish. In short, the average popularizer addresses himself to 'the child in all of us' – meaning some maimed and dwarfish version of himself (dwarfish enough to begin with, too often) with all his sharpest faculties and keenest sensibilities, as well as all his education, lopped off. Isaac Azimov has done some good work in science-for-the-layman, but there are times when he makes me feel I am curled up in my cradle, and a twinkly man in a white coat is teaching me to count – 'one . . . two . . . that's right' by pinching my little fingers one after the other. He may stand as a symbol of all those who make this kind of mistake.

These are, in fact, failures in popularization itself; they put off the plainest 'plain man' the writer thinks he is addressing. 'Humanization' (forgive the word) is obliged to appeal also to some education in the reader, some store of information, interests, and experience of a specifically intellectual kind. The writer must take for granted and make use of this education in explaining his new subject. He will use the fact that, for instance, his reader knows what *kind* of poetry T. S. Eliot writes, and D. H. Lawrence's kind of novel, and something about Kafka, and Proust. He will use his reader's experience in tracing analogies, in seeing likenesses and differences, in following an argument, in distinguishing relevant from irrelevant evidence, theories from hypotheses, and a case of intellectual debt from one of equal participation in an intellectual milieu. In short, he will assume that his reader also belongs to the Western intellectual tradition, though to a different branch of it. And by doing so, he will, in fact, bring that tradition into existence as a social fact; which is just what we are reading these books for. The non-existence of that tradition as a social fact is another name for the split between the two cultures.

The specifically humanist failures in science-for-the-layman do not spring so readily to mind, because so few writers have attempted humanism. But some British men of science make their gesture to the reader's other interests with a Latin tag, or a quotation from 'The Grammarian's Funeral', and with some courtly but palsied graces of style imitated from the essays of Charles Lamb. These are not successful appeals to the modern reader's sense of the community between all educated men. But they are attempts, or ghosts of attempts, to create that community, and so shame the inhumane world into which they survive.

For if there is a humanism of science today it is at best the social-conscience humanism of science feeding a hungry world, or science repenting the atom bomb. Social-conscience humanism can, of course, inspire some valuable books, but it cannot satisfy the layman's fear that its explanations are not really science; they are bound to remain an application of science, and the books a higher journalism. But neither are the textbooks the real thing, for the lay reader, even if he does the problems at the ends of the chapters. What we are looking for is something between and beyond those two.

There are, of course, some liberally conceived textbooks (Gerald Holton's introductory physics course is an excellent example) which are worth working through. There are the works of the great men themselves, the *Discours de la Méthode*, the *Dialogues Concerning Two New Sciences*, the *Opticks*. There are classics of the past, like Tyndall's life of Faraday, in which the scientific work is explained alongside, and in some connection with, the man's personality. All these kinds of books are worth reading; the last has every advantage except compeers. But none of them can be the mainstay of someone trying to translate himself from a state of illiteracy in science to a minimal, franchise-winning numeracy. There are, in fact, many books which interest and satisfy an adult reader while explaining scientific ideas and methods. But it is another, minor, effect of the modern breakdown that one cannot find those books; that the humanist seeking instruction stumbles into an endless morass, an Okeefinokee of unreadable, unrewarding, or unendurably condescending explication, with no trustworthy guide to the firm islands of humanism. Publishers, even those who specialize in this line, issue books of every variety of quality. Blurb-writers, and even reviewers, use no reliable vocabulary to indicate the mental or educational level of a book's intended readers. The 'libraries' of such books include every sort of thing, quite undepartmentalized.

One must make an exception for *The Scientific American*; its articles, its reviews of other books (these are particularly useful), and its series of Scientific American books. But even that exception is only partial. The magazine is written for scientists, though not for specialists; one needs some university work in science to read it; its articles are often rather stodgy and overtechnical; above all, they don't appeal enough to the reader's non-scientific interests. And something of the same kind applies to the books made up from those articles. One should also mention the Science Study series of books written for the Physical Science Study Committee set up at M.I.T., and operating from Watertown, Massachusetts. This series has achieved more consistency than any other. You know when you pick up a new volume how much it will expect from you, and you expect from it a high standard of explication. What else you may expect from it, however, is quite professedly not the humanism I have been describing. These books are intended for the 'young' 'Student'; the mature layman may also read, and if he does he will find more that stimulates and satisfies him than in most books that profess to have him in mind; but he will be listening from the back of the class, listening through other people's ears. And there is nothing in England – that I can discover – to equal these two American series. (These are my impressions after some years of semi-systematic browsing, but without a comprehensive survey; it may be that there are publishers and 'libraries' to which I am unjust in these paragraphs.)

Now let us consider some of those books that do shape their message to our ears. First, the type whose best examples are Selig Hecht's *Explaining the Atom* and Fred Hoyle's *The Universe Around Us*. These are properly speaking examples of popularization rather than humanization; because the reader they have in mind is a plain man. But he is the best version of that; a man who worries intelligently about the uses of atomic power, who wants to understand whatever affects him, who looks at the night sky, who is excited by the numbers and sizes of astronomy. He is far from the plain man so often conjured up for us, who knows nothing and has no interests, and is, in fact, the writer minus every feature for which he respects himself. Hecht's reader is much closer to the educated layman of humanization. And these books are also quite superb explication. And ideas are made vivid, clear, and lively.

Explication is too often taken to be the whole content (serious content) of science-for-the-layman; so that I have here stressed other things. But it is, of course, of prime importance; and very rare; and, if it is good enough, it takes the place of everything else. I mean that if a writer explains something difficult with perfect clarity, brevity, energy, and relevance, then the most sophisticated reader is completely satisfied, and needs no reference to other interests. When, for instance, George Gamow takes a chapter off from his main argument (in his book on gravity) to explain calculus to the unmathematical reader, the audacity and the pace of the whole enterprise reassure the reader that he is not being condescended to. They even reassure him against some of Dr Gamow's jokes. Irving Adler is perhaps the best example of pure explication. His *The New Mathematics* could hardly be improved as a piece of clarity, simplicity, accuracy, and readability. But it doesn't offer to be even popularization in the full sense, because it doesn't relate its instruction to the reader's other concerns, as Hecht and Hoyle do. George Gamow could perhaps be put beside the latter, but he is such a personal performer that he needs qualifying comments. He appeals to a less serious reader;

he appeals to an audience, in fact. The reader makes his intellectual efforts between draughts of pretty farcical humour, and pretty frank self-display. It is a vaudeville performance more than a piece of teaching, though one involving first-class abilities.

Then there is the kind of book Rachel Carson writes. *The Sea Around Us* and *The Silent Spring* offer us a great deal of information, and in connection with our political and our poetical concerns. This is not, however, the humanism I mean, because the books are too obviously best-sellers; they handle their non-scientific themes in the manner of serious journalism, not from inside the discipline; the poetical parts, for instance, are not going to satisfy the literary reader. But, of course, we could do with many more books like these. They form an important part of the literature of science. There has always been a tradition of this kind of humanism (evoking now the word's humanitarian and also its poetical senses) in the sciences of botany, zoology, physiology, etc. – the life sciences. In fact, many non-scientists, some who even think themselves anti-scientific, are keen students of nature in one or other of these forms. They have identified science with physics – as, of course, have many physicists – and so *both* deny the rank of science to biology *and* the connection with nature to physics. This spotlights for us once again the narrowing effect of our modern misconception of science.

It is when we come to the work of J. G. Crowther that we get within sight of the humanism I have described. He has written a lot of science-for-the-layman, and the books I refer to here are just those in his series, British Men of Science. His method is broadly biographical, but in each book he deals with a group of men who taken together represent a period. (This is not true of *Francis Bacon*; and perhaps in consequence it is a less successful book.) Crowther is a Marxist, and he examines each scientist for the economic motives and consequences of his work, both in his personal life and in the life of the society to which he belonged; the economic motives and consequences, and their ideological affiliations. Some Marxist crudities of style and method make attribution of humanism to these books a paradox at first; the interpretation of history follows an uninspired pattern; but the case studies are both sensible and interesting. The volumes dealing with the seventeenth century and with the Industrial Revolution give the reader a convincing picture of the men, a clear account of their work and a wide-ranging theory of the relation of both to the general forces operating in the society of the time. In the second of those two he puts together Henry Cavendish's research, James Watt's career, the Edinburgh circle of savants, the Birmingham of Matthew Boulton and Erasmus Darwin, and, through Priestley, the whole ferment of radical ideas. For anyone brought up on the conventional accounts of parliaments and ministries, this is a most exciting piece of history; and one in which scientific exposition plays a radical part; in other words, a humanistic example of science-for-the-layman.

Then there are other ways of approaching scientific exposition, which I have not yet found successfully translated into book-length treatment, but of which there are some very exciting glimpses. The organization of science, for instance, is a subject which appears from time to time in novels (not often those by novelists who take their art most seriously), but which deserves full-length non-fictional treatment. One would like to know *how* famous joint discoveries of the past were made; how a great laboratory director like Rutherford operated; how individual temperament interacts with the scientific method; how a project transforms itself in the right hands; how enthusiasm is built up; how financial backing is won; how and where the moral sense operates; and so on. Our ideas and our information on these subjects are tainted by their association with television serials and with bedside-reading novels. We need a more reliable account of them.

We need books about great scientific events, linking them with contemporary events in other intellectual disciplines. For instance, a very interesting book could be written about Einstein's work on the General Theory of Relativity, comparing it with D. H. Lawrence's contemporary work on *Women in Love*. Such a book would describe and explain in turn each man's achievement, in its setting of previous literary or scientific history, but also in its setting of subsequent developments. It would also describe the two men's personalities and careers; with primary stress on the intellectual aspects in each case, but quite freely exploring beyond that to present a complete picture. It could also describe the European scene that divided Einstein's Switzerland from Lawrence's Cornwall in 1916; the slaughter on the Somme. Here are three of the crucial factors in modern history, to be brought into relation. There is no need for any striking moral – either likenesses or differences between the two – to emerge from the comparison. One would at least expect, before investigation, to find some interesting contrasts between the contemporary professional treatment of the General Theory and that of *Women in Love*. But to make an interesting book all that is needed is that each should be fully presented in its historical setting as an achievement of the Western intellectual tradition.

We need a book about each of those striking historical coincidences in the history of science. For instance, the invention of non-Euclidean geometry by Gauss, Lobachevsky, and Bolyai, each working independently, and all within a decade or so. Or the case of Caspar Wessel and Jean-Robert Argand, both of whom worked out the beautiful geometrical interpretation of imaginary numbers, in total ignorance of each other, and one seven years after the other. There is an historical drama in each case; so many centuries without this idea, these minds living without contact with each other, without much similarity, but in response to the same historical forces, gradually growing into the same activity, finally making the same discovery. We need a book about each of those great disputations over terms; for instance, the debate about 'power', 'force' and 'energy' in the mid-nineteenth century, between Carnot, Joule, Thompson, and Helmholtz. It would be interesting to see the likeness and difference, in detail, between such debates and literary quarrels over classic and romantic. We need books to follow up the clue offered in these words by Claude Bernard in his *Introduction to the Study of Experimental Medicine*:

In scientific investigation, minutiae of method are of the highest importance. The happy choice of an animal, an instrument constructed in some special way, one reagent used instead of another, may often suffice to solve the most abstract and lofty questions. In a word, the greatest scientific truths are rooted in details of experimental investigation, which form, as it were, the soil in which these truths develop.

Finally, the idea of the limits of different sciences, and the changes of those limits with the passing of time, also offers a lot of scope. There is the advance of the idea of mechanics from Galileo to Newton to Boyle, and so on, supplanting with its explanations those earlier theories which had kept the stars, or the earth, or the plants, parts of some quite different branch of knowledge. To which must be added the retreats of that idea from areas it was not, after all, competent to explain; the retreat from Descartes' version of the human body as a crude mechanical system, for example, with nerve tubes filled with a compressible fluid. These to-and-fro shiftings of ideas can be very vivid if one has examples from non-scientists as well as scientists, and are particularly interesting cases of intellectual history. Magnus Pyke has a book on this subject, but there is room for more than one other.

But approaches to science-for-the-layman which seem *un*-promising include the limits of science in the other sense. No one now needs to have it proved to him that science does not bring us only advantages; and yet new books hustle from the presses hot with this message. Nor do we need it proved that scientists deal in 'how' but not 'why'; and yet Latin teachers regularly devote a year or two of their retirement to its demonstration. Of course, one cannot lay down such laws without loopholes, tomorrow a book along these lines might appear which would engage our attention; but it seems worth warning prospective writers and publishers against the effort. Nor are external analogies between the arts and the sciences likely to be profitable. The magic of 'relativity' has been much invoked in this shady cause; non-Euclidean geometry has been supposed to have something in common with non-metrical verse; and the new physics has been supposed to offer evidence that men have free will. Lawrence Durrell has some fine specimens of this sort of thing in the *Alexandria Quartet*. The only analogies between the arts and the sciences worth making are those which reveal their common origin in the Western intellectual tradition, their common function as modes of intellection. The contemporary operational procedures of the two – even the contemporary philosophical problems these bring up – will be only accidentally and trivially parallel.

But the book I most want to see written I have not yet described. We most need studies of scientists which will make clear the outline of their intellectual personalities; not the man as opposed to the scientist, nor the story of his laboratory work as opposed to his private life, but a third idea which will combine something of both alternatives in each case. What the layman wants to understand is how a given psychological factor (within the total complex) is related to (expresses itself in, is encouraged by, is in conflict with) the kind of scientific work done. F. W. Aston, we are told, was a neat, prim bachelor, devoted to his hobbies, who early became what is called oldmaidish in his general way of life. And his scientific work consisted of finer and finer measurements in the mass-spectrograph he designed and built himself. Nearly all his scientific life was passed in one room of the Cavendish, where, alone, without assistants or colleagues, he designed and constructed and used his machine, took it to pieces and built another, and then improved it again. This is not 'just science' nor even just physics; it is a certain kind of physics; which he *chose* to do. His scientific achievement is obviously just as closely related to his nature, his psychological endowment and what he made of that, as, for instance, Gray's or Pope's literary achievement was. When we discuss Pope, we put the poems in the context of the man, his education, his interests, his handicaps, his special talents; except when we are engaged in some pure critical exercise. It both derives from and reinforces our misconception of science that we don't do the same with Aston.

Michelson, to take another example, was also a measurer and machine-builder, but of a much harsher, more arrogant and domineering, more aggressively masculine type, often in conflict with his colleagues. Pasteur, almost the opposite, was a kindly, idealistic civil-servant type, devoted to his parents, his children, his people, his country; and (obviously, in some sense 'therefore') he spent *his* scientific life on problems of preventing disease and controlling infection and improving industry. These examples are rather crude. I mean only to establish a principle, the full operation of which explains the character, the contour, the flavour, of nearly every piece of scientific work. It explains science as the expression of human personality in the same sense as art, politics, history, philosophy are that. Put beside Michelson James Joyce, and beside Pasteur Mark Twain. No one in practice appreciates Joyce's or Twain's work without some reference to the man who created it – and to the social forces which created him. No one in practice says, 'As for Twain's work, that was Art, so don't try to explain that to me – anyway, that's got nothing to do with his personality.' Twain and his books and the America in which he lived are intimately connected in our minds (we must be ready on occasion to distinguish them, of course), and it is because they are that literature is one of the humanities. When we realize that the same is true of Michelson, science will have entered the humanities, too.

The only book I know which does this job is Koestler's biography of Kepler. It shows in fullest detail how Kepler's temperament, interests, adventures, beliefs, expressed themselves in his scientific work. Not only how they hampered or rivalled or paralleled it, but how they shaped it; his choice of subjects to investigate, his way of working, his way of publishing, even his actual discoveries. If you cut away all reference to his temperament, interests, adventures, beliefs, his scientific career becomes an abstract scheme which gives no idea of the facts. One sees quite clearly in this book how inadequate is that old myth of a scientific method into which a man steps as on to an escalator, and which then carries him smoothly up to his destination – while all *his* efforts are directed to not being unscientific, not doing handsprings on the escalator. No one could have been more unscientific than Kepler; and it was his handsprings, as much as other things, which led to his great achievements. Obviously, then, a scientist's emotional discipline is not restricted to not falling in love with the lab. technician, or not getting jealous of a colleague, or not signing on with the Kremlin. It was the whole man who worked out the orbit of Mars; all sorts of ideological and personal loyalties both drove him to the task and determined how he did it. It is only a whole man's successful self-discipline that can be called the scientific method; it is not a suit of armour into which anyone can pop, and thereafter need only hold his breath.

One may think that Koestler had an easy job to demonstrate this thesis on Kepler, who was such a rich, eccentric, poetic personality. But as soon as one starts looking at opposite types, what strikes one is that they are all easy, for opposite reasons. When one has been shown one case of the temperament shaping the work, they all seem to cry out for that explanation. Newton is a fair example of an opposite type; but how much there is to be explained temperamentally, in those two bursts of fantastically concentrated work on gravitation, the almost equally fantastic eighteen-year lapse between, the fierce resentment and evasion of possible criticism, the frigid refusal of equal relationship or co-operation with anyone. There is an extraordinary temperament there, both very direct and very evasive, and it affected the work done, in choice of subject, relationship to other workers, manner of publication (and non-publication), and style of work. The style expressed the man in Newton's work as much as in Milton's: the simple perfection of his experimental style, the lofty archaism of both language and mathematics in the *Principia*, the stiff, impersonal, official style he imposed on the Royal Society, and through that on all British science. The *Principia is* Newton as much as *Paradise Lost* is Milton; and it is late-seventeenth-century England just as much. Both these characters are accessible to the understanding of the humanist, once the scientific technicalities are explained; and they are no more difficult than those Koestler explained in *The Watershed*. And when Newton, and Lavoisier, and Rutherford, are made as much personalities to us as Milton, and Wordsworth, and Sartre, then the humanist will find that he can indeed 'move into and out of science as he can the other fields of knowledge', and that science *is* one of the humanities.

One mistake that is often made in arguing that science is one of the humanities, in presenting it to non-scientists, is to insist on its irrationalities. The real romance of science is its rationalizing power. The mark of the philistine, in any branch of knowledge, is surely not rigidity of conception so much as relativism. All things seem equally possible to him, there is no hierarchy among his ideas, and consequently he can invest no emotions (only vague and unformed feelings) in those ideas. At least this is true of the literary *man, in his dealings with all branches of knowledge in which he is not expert. He is very able to imagine, for instance, brilliant ways of making a fortune. What he cannot imagine is that some of them will work and some won't; much less that you can know which are which in advance. The romance of finance is the rationalization of this vague realm of possibilities. Of course, the first and simplest kind of romance is the extraordinary, the inexplicable, case. But the second kind, which better satisfies the adult mind, is the revelation of order in what seemed congenital disorder. And we may suppose that to some molecular physicists dozens of wildly unequal possibilities, in literature's special realm of personal relations and aesthetic taste, all seem equally plausible. In presenting any branch of knowledge to intelligent laymen, it is its power of explanation that must be focused, not its inexplicabilities, its mysteries, its muddles.*

It is useful, of course, to rescue any branch of human endeavour from an image so mechanistic and infallibilistic as that science has cursed itself with. The story of Blondlot and his N-rays is a very valuable chapter in any history of science. But it is not useful to insist on, for instance, the uncertainty principle, as if that added the touch of poetry, mystery, romance, which could reconcile the literary man to science. The real romance of science is its certainty. For a non-scientist, the exciting thing is to realize that one can measure *the weight of the atmosphere above us – that there is a calculable, predictable, constant difference between atmospheric pressure on a mountain peak, and at sea-level – that there* is *such a thing as sea-level all over the world. The literary imagination assents readily to the proposition that air obeys gravity; it is quite ready to suppose far wilder things – that it obeys levity at the same time. The exciting scientific achievement is to follow through this insight, this possibility, and work out how* much *air weighs, and how* much *air there must therefore be above us, and that levity is not a scientific fact. The literary man instinctively presupposes that there will always be so many variables (the temperature of the air, its state of compression, its chemical composition, its height, its movement) that one could not make reliable comparative statements. Science extends the power of the mind out through these misty regions; which are essentially just as misty for literary people today as they were for the contemporaries of Galileo or*

Aristotle. It is the act of clarification, of simplification and solidification of that shifting, multiform half-knowledge, which is the romance of science. Writers and teachers should aim to rehearse such an act for us as dramatically as possible; present to us two or three equally plausible propositions about some phenomenon of common experience – the way coal burns or birds fly – and then show how we know which is true, and how knowing that enables us to know and do other things.

7. Conclusion

The set of practical problems we refer to as the two cultures (never mind the set of ideological and personal loyalties involved) is so tangled that it is difficult to make any satisfying statement about it. There is the political problem, the educational problem, the communications problem, the cultural problem proper, problems special to the literary culture, problems special to the scientific culture, and so on. A general statement which is true from one of those points of view may be untrue from another; one must spend a lot of time saying what one is not talking about, or defining one's terms so narrowly as to have that effect.

Moreover, one can easily lose one's track in the argument even after having found it. One separates off a group of problems for investigation; in my case, those special to the literary culture; but in investigating them I am inevitably led back to consider, briefly, partially, things like the communications problem, the nature of culture, the nature of science, even some of the problems special to the scientific culture. This is necessary in order to make sense, and also in order to give due emphasis. For those qualified and sinuous generalizations which do not shipwreck on some contrary truth are not very weighty or urgent unless you read them from several different viewpoints at the same time. That the student of modern literature may become socially disaffected is important because there is also a general tendency to believe the arts' social pronouncements, and because thoes pronouncements are passionately true in some sense, and because his disaffection widens the gap between the artist and the hardworking, socially conscientious part of society, and so on, and so on. The problem as a whole is dramatically important, and must be discussed as if it were; but in proving it to exist one must so isolate each aspect that what one has proved after each successful argument may seem trivial. The arguer is forced to connect afterwards rather separate reasonings. It is therefore hard for him, and harder for a reader, to maintain a sense of relevance, of logical rigour, or indeed of any progress in the argument.

I think this is why, when I have tried to tell people what I have been doing these four years, I have often met a puzzled dissatisfaction, and the question, 'Well, what have you got out of it? What has it done for you?' This may be the reaction of some readers of the book; it must be part of the response of all, however well I have succeeded; so I must try to answer it here.

I have not, I should be clear, acquired a great deal of scientific information. I have even more definitely not acquired a scientific education; what I do know remains a collection of scraps and pious generalities; I still have to learn things several times over, exerting far more voluntary attention than I do (with much harder problems) in my own subject. I cannot claim even that 'minimal, franchise-winning numeracy' I set out for.

Nor can I claim to have redressed the temperamental imbalance of my intellectual training. Mine is congenitally now a literary mind; its best thinking will always be done as a fragment, a servant, a healthy-as-possible specimen of the general literary mind. When one realizes the relation of that mind to a wider intellectual tradition, one inevitably pays more attention to the forms of demonstration; to definition, proposition, evidence, reasoning; but that cannot be said to affect temperament, because it has more to do with how one convinces others than how one convinces oneself. This book is as literary in form and feeling as A Mirror for Anglo-Saxons.

I have, of course, made up my mind about the various formulations of this particular problem. I now know why, for instance, the sentences by Auden which I use as epigraphs strike me as both true and inadequate. True because of the force and complexity of the attitudes they symbolize; inadequate because of their contented resting in epigram and paradox; a paradox of feeling as much as of thought. One need not feel mainly like a shabby curate facing dukes when one is in the company of scientists; there is a potential brotherhood in the relationship, too, and that only seems so potential and hypothetical because we are hypnotized by our theories of culture, of science, of literature. Nor are the deeds of scientists 'speechless'. If we had the right biographies of Einstein, the poet could celebrate his achievement, even its specifically scientific significance, as easily as the statesman's, the soldier's, or another writer's. The Manhattan Project is a subject for legend and myth quite comparable with, say, the Pilgrim Fathers' voyage. It only seems incomparable to Auden because our culture has created a barrier, emotional and intellectual, between the non-scientist and science.

But merely to make up one's mind about other people's conundrums, however tantalizing, or even merely to have made a reasoned statement of one's own case, would be something of an anti-climax. There are also the modifications of quite general attitudes.

First of all, I have satisfied myself that a problem does exist for literary people, and exists in the shape and proportions Snow described. This is very important, since so many people have denied it in print, and even more in conversation; or have so confused the different issues that the whole controversy has come to seem unprofitable. As long as its mere existence is so smoothly refuted, so easily ignored, all thinking about its solution will be choked to death in preliminaries and wild irrelevancies. That is why I have rather insisted on things like 'the literary mind' (its differences from the scientific) throughout the book, piling up ever new evidence, finding everywhere new confirmation. This problem is only one of those Snow discusses, but it is perhaps better described in the plural, as all the handicaps with which a literary education may endow its products, handicaps of emotion and understanding, derived from the anti-scientific myth; so named, clearly grasped, this is a most important idea for anyone who is literary.

Second, I have understood why I was as it were compelled to outreach myself in A Mirror for Anglo-Saxons. *Not that this was a simply logical error, from which anyone could recover merely by taking thought, by adjusting his premises or his reasoning. Like so many of the paradoxes generated by this conflict, this roots itself in those instinctive preferences and enthusiasms and indifferences, to change which would be to change oneself. The split between the cultures, the death of humanism, has bequeathed to literature, especially in England, the responsibility of doing humanism's work for it, of regulating a whole national culture. This has happened especially in England because there the anti-humanist strain of modern literature has compensated for itself most vigorously; all the great modern writers are priests of personal freedom, but Lawrence and Leavis are priests of organic social order, too. This is a magnificent tradition and training to inherit, but the pride of responsibility brings with it stresses which can be destructive, intellectually and emotionally, if they are not understood.*

Most important, this investigation has made clear to me the ideal at least of a more complex attentiveness, a fuller intellectual patience, answering to that larger structure of relevant truth I now acknowledge – relevant to those faculties of choice and attentiveness and love which form the main arteries of our moral life – a structure within which I see my own insights mesh with others that are not mine. I see roughly where the things I know fit in with the things I don't, and what my contribution to the more inclusive and ultimate judgements ought to be. This is a structure and a relevance much larger than I could believe in before. It remains ideal and theoretical in part because it would have to exist in other people's minds, too, and their books, before it could be actualized in mine. But along and around it that combination of interests we could call a new humanism could grow.